USBORNE SCIENCE & EXPERIMENTS
ECOLOGY

Richard Spurgeon

Edited by Corinne Stockley

Designed by Stephen Wright

Illustrated by
Kuo Kang Chen, Brin Edwards and Caroline Ewen

Scientific advisor: Dr. Margaret Rostron

Contents

3   About this book
4   What is ecology?
6   The environment
8   Ecosystems
10 The ocean
12 Cycles in nature
14 Disturbing the cycles
16 Adaptation
18 Coniferous and deciduous forests
20 Relationships in nature
22 Population and conservation
24 Urban ecosystems
26 Tropical rainforests
28 Change in nature
30 Evolution
32 People and planet
33 Energy and the environment
34 The future

Ecology projects:

36   Building an ant observatory
     Making a pond
38   Building a compost heap
     Sprouting beans and seeds
39   Building a bird table
     Birdwatching
40   Planting trees
42   Making recycled paper
     A windowsill salad garden
     Organizing your own group
44 Going further
46 Glossary
48 Index

Copyright © 1988 Usborne Publishing Ltd.

The name Usborne and the device ⌐ are Trade Marks of Usborne Publishing Ltd.

Printed in Spain. American edition 1988.

About this book

Ecology is the study of all living things and how they work with each other and the world around them. This book shows how plants, animals and their environments are all linked together in one vast web, and how we ourselves are all part of this web. It explains the basic terms and ideas of ecology, using examples from the very different ecological regions of the world.

Using the glossary

The glossary on pages 46-47 is a useful reference point. It brings together and explains all the main ecological terms used in the book.

Useful addresses

If you want to get more involved in helping wildlife and improving the environment, or just want to find out more about what other people are doing, you can turn to pages 44-45. These have a list of addresses of leading conservation and environmental groups. Many of these organizations run activities for young people, and all of them will send you more information.

Throughout this book, there are many examples of how the things people are doing today are causing problems and disturbances in the natural world. At the same time, there are suggestions as to what can be done to help. These range from activities which will help you improve the situation in your local area, to some ideas about how the larger scale problems could be solved.

This scene shows one of the harshest of the world's environments, and some of the people and animals adapted to survive there. You can find out more about the ecology of the world's deserts on pages 16-17.

Activities and projects

Special boxes like this one are used for activities, experiments and projects. They are found throughout the main part of the book, as well as in the "Ecology projects" section at the back (most of the projects in this section take more time and effort).

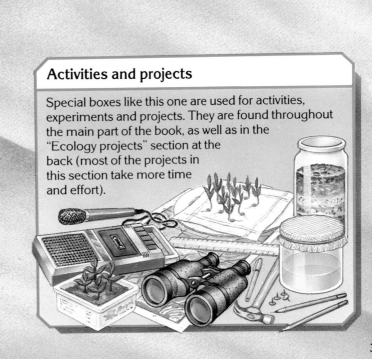

What is ecology?

Ecology is the study of living things in their natural surroundings, or **environment**. This is everything, living and non-living, that is around them.

Your own environment is made up of all that you can see and much that you can't when you look around you. Its basic features stay very much the same, e.g. the air that you breathe, but the details are constantly changing.

Your body is an environment, too. Inside you there are thousands of tiny living things, like bacteria that help you digest your food. Their environment is your body.

Large intestine

A sample of bacteria taken from the large intestine.

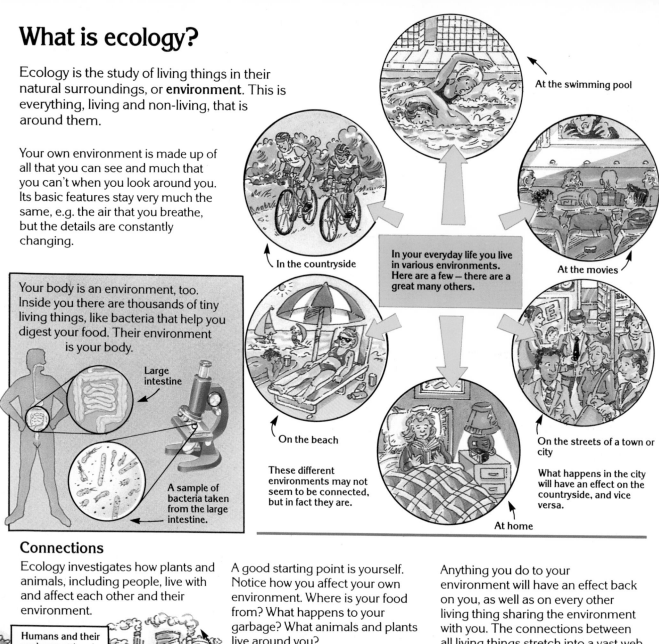

In your everyday life you live in various environments. Here are a few — there are a great many others.

At the swimming pool

In the countryside

At the movies

On the beach

On the streets of a town or city

What happens in the city will have an effect on the countryside, and vice versa.

At home

These different environments may not seem to be connected, but in fact they are.

Connections

Ecology investigates how plants and animals, including people, live with and affect each other and their environment.

A good starting point is yourself. Notice how you affect your own environment. Where is your food from? What happens to your garbage? What animals and plants live around you?

Anything you do to your environment will have an effect back on you, as well as on every other living thing sharing the environment with you. The connections between all living things stretch into a vast web.

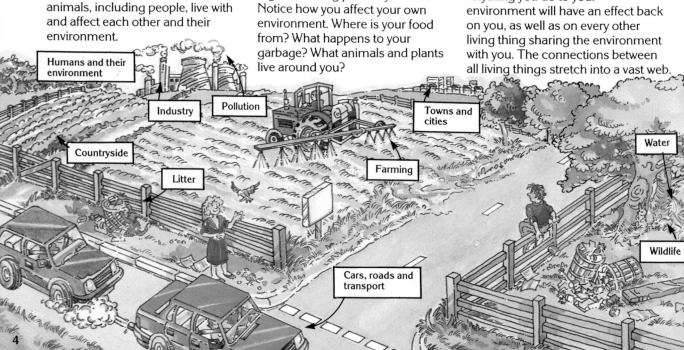

Humans and their environment

Industry

Pollution

Countryside

Litter

Towns and cities

Farming

Water

Wildlife

Cars, roads and transport

Habitats

The natural home of a group of plants and animals is called a **habitat** and the group of plants and animals which live there is a **community**. Lift up a stone and see what lives in the habitat underneath it.

Smaller habitats are part of larger habitats. The stone may be at the side of a stream, which may be in a wood. A different, larger community lives in each larger habitat.

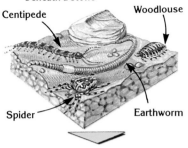

Community of animals living beneath a stone

Centipede
Woodlouse
Spider
Earthworm

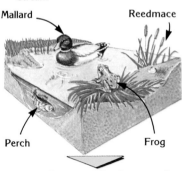

Part of community living by or in a stream

Mallard
Reedmace
Perch
Frog

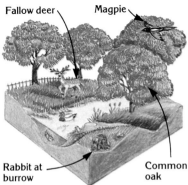

Part of open woodland community

Fallow deer
Magpie
Rabbit at burrow
Common oak

Try to find some different habitats in your area. Look everywhere – in, on, under and around. But remember to leave everything as you found it.

A freshwater pond

A pond is a good example of a larger habitat. It is the home of a large community of different plants and animals. The pond, its community, and the non-living environment around it, make up a complete ecological unit, called an **ecosystem**. For more on ecosystems and how they work, see page 8.

Pond-dipping is a good way of studying the pond community. Gently drag a net through different areas of the pond. Make notes on what you find. Put anything interesting into a container for closer inspection (you could use a book on pond life for identification). Don't forget to put everything back into the pond when you have finished.

You can either buy a net or make your own. Get a metal coat-hanger and bend it into a circle. Stick the ends into a long piece of bamboo, or tie them to a pole, and tie an old stocking to the rim.

A home-made net
Tie a knot in the stocking and cut off the excess.
Tie the stocking to the rim with string.

Ponds are much less common today than they were forty years ago. Many have been filled in or have grown over. This is most unfortunate for their inhabitants. Some plants and animals only live in certain habitats. When these disappear, so do they.

Build your own pond

You can help the wildlife in your area by building a pond. This will attract all sorts of wildlife and is not too hard to do. See pages 36-37 for instructions on how to make, stock and maintain a pond.

A man-made pond

Dragonfly
Marsh marigold
Water lily
Frog
Common newt
Pond skater
Yellowflag
Canadian pondweed
Ram's horn snail

This is how your pond might look when it is finished. It will take quite a bit of work and time, and must be properly looked after, but once it is established many animals will come to visit or stay and you will be able to study them whenever you want.

A home-made underwater viewer will give you a better view of pond life. Carefully cut the top and bottom off a plastic squeezy bottle. Cover one end with clear plastic wrap and attach it with a rubber band. Place it in the water and look through the open end (for safety, cover the cut edge with tape).

Underwater viewer

The environment

As well as influencing our environment, we are constantly being influenced by it. Like all living things, we are dependent on our environment for the essentials of life.

The basis of all life on earth is the sun. Without its heat the world would be a frozen mass of lifeless rock and ice. It provides plants and animals with the energy they need to live. It generates the winds by heating the earth's land masses and the air above them, and drives the water cycle by evaporating water into the atmosphere (see page 12). It is the most vital component of the environment, without which life on earth could not exist.

The climate

This map shows the world's six major climates. The main influences on the climate are: distance from the Equator, distance from the ocean (it is drier inland), and the height above sea level (the higher you go, the colder it gets)

Living things are greatly affected by the conditions around them. The temperature, rainfall and other aspects of the climate in an area influence the forms, growth and behavior of the plants and animals found there (see map on page 8).

The climate and the earth's landscape interact to create the larger environment within which life can exist. Over time, the powerful weathering effects of the climate have formed the earth's life-supporting soil.

The sun's energy is not evenly spread across the surface of the earth. Equatorial areas receive far more than polar areas. This imbalance creates and drives the winds around the world.

At the poles, the sun's rays pass through more atmosphere and are spread over a larger land surface than at the Equator, so it is much colder.

The interactions of warm winds and ocean currents from the tropical areas and cold winds and currents from polar regions cause climatic variations wherever they converge.

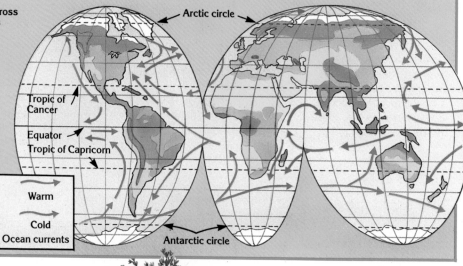

Arctic circle

Tropic of Cancer

Equator
Tropic of Capricorn

Antarctic circle

Climate key
- Polar
- Mountain
- Cold forest
- Temperate
- Dry
- Equatorial
- Sub-equatorial

Warm

Cold

Ocean currents

The importance of soil

The weathering effects of temperature, wind and water break down the rocks of the earth's surface to produce mineral particles which are the basis of soil. For more about the changing landscape, see page 28.

Tiny plants grow on these rock particles, die and decompose to form organic matter called **humus**. This mixture of mineral particles and organic matter is what makes up soil. Soil also contains water and air, trapped between the particles, and millions of microscopic organisms, like bacteria, as well as insects and some larger animals.

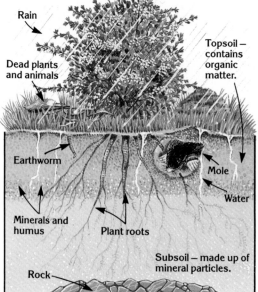

Rain

Dead plants and animals

Topsoil – contains organic matter.

Earthworm

Mole

Water

Minerals and humus

Plant roots

Subsoil – made up of mineral particles.

Rock

There are many types of soil, each with a different ratio of humus and minerals (and different types of mineral particles, formed from the breakdown of different rocks). Each type of soil supports its own range of plant species.

Soil supplies many of the essential needs of most green plants. It is the source of their water, the minerals they need to develop, and gives them a solid base in which their roots can grow.

Soil experiments

To see what soil is made of, take a sample and shake it up in a jar of water. Let it settle for a few days, then study the different layers.

Humus – organic matter

Clay – mainly aluminum silicate

Silt – mud formed from tiny pieces of rock

Sand – mainly silica

Gravel – larger rock particles

Now get samples of different types of soil from a variety of places. Do the same thing to each and compare the results.

To see what sort of animals are living in the soil, take a sample and put it on a piece of gauze in a funnel. Place this on a tall jar under a lamp overnight. The light and heat will force the creatures down into the jar.

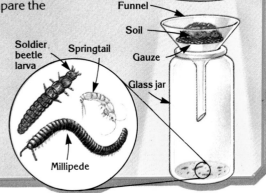

Soldier beetle larva

Springtail

Millipede

Lamp

Funnel

Soil

Gauze

Glass jar

Soil erosion

Most of the earth's surface is covered by a layer of soil, ranging from $1/4$ in thick mountainous regions to $6\frac{1}{2}$ ft in cultivated areas. We all depend on this thin layer for our food supplies, yet everywhere it is threatened by soil erosion.

Over-grazing, poor irrigation, intensive farming and the destruction of tree cover mean that vital topsoil is left exposed, and much is being blown or washed away. If this continues, we may not have enough fertile land left to grow enough food.

In the early 1930s, farming areas in the American mid-west were devastated by soil erosion.

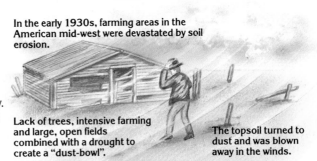

Lack of trees, intensive farming and large, open fields combined with a drought to create a "dust-bowl".

The topsoil turned to dust and was blown away in the winds.

Energy for life

All living things need energy for their growth, movement and life processes. The source of this energy is the sun.

Green plants use the sun's energy to build their own food from the simpler elements around them. They are called **producers**. They use the sunlight in a process called **photosynthesis** to convert water and carbon dioxide into oxygen and carbohydrates. Some of the carbohydrates are then combined with minerals from the soil and used for growth, others form a store of food (mainly in leaves), to provide energy when needed. Animals cannot produce their own food. They depend on the food stored in plants to give them energy for life and so are called **consumers**.

Process of photosynthesis

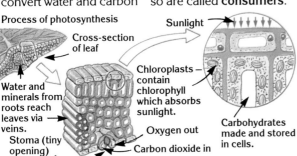

Cross-section of leaf

Sunlight

Water and minerals from roots reach leaves via veins.

Stoma (tiny opening)

Chloroplasts – contain chlorophyll which absorbs sunlight.

Oxygen out

Carbon dioxide in

Carbohydrates made and stored in cells.

Plant experiments

Put some cress seeds in two dishes lined with damp kitchen paper. Put both in a dark cupboard for one or two days, then take one out and put it by a window. After a few more days you will see how important sunlight is for healthy plant growth.

Add some food dye to the water you give the healthy cress. Study what happens. The plants draw up the water like they would from soil.

Plants move their leaves to catch the most light. Study the growth of a plant in a sunny place, then turn it round and see what happens.

Dish from cupboard

Unhealthy cress plants

Keep the paper damp all the time.

Dish from windowsill

Healthy cress plants

Ecosystems

An ecosystem consists of a given habitat and its community. The living things within it interact with each other and their non-living (**abiotic**) environment to form an ecological unit which is largely self-contained.

Many smaller ecosystems can be found within larger ones, like a rotting tree branch, within a wood.

Biomes are the largest ecosystems into which the earth's land surface can be divided (see right). They are named after the main type of vegetation found there, and each one is home to a very large variety of plants and animals.

○ Ice
● Mountain
◐ Maquis. Warm, wet winters, hot, dry summers, scrubland.
◐ Tropical forest. Hot and wet, with a great diversity of life, e.g. monkeys and exotic birds.

◐ Desert. Extremes of temperature, little rain, scarcity of life.
◐ Deciduous forest. Warm summers, cold winters, mainly deciduous woodland (e.g. oak or beech), variety of animals.

◐ Savannah (tropical grassland) – hot with wet winters, open plains with trees, antelopes.
● Coniferous forest. Cold all year, dominated by forests of conifers (e.g. spruce and pine), deer and wolves.

● Temperate grassland. Hot summers, cold winters, open grassy plains with buffalo.
○ Tundra. Very cold, windy and treeless, little animal life.

The climate of each biome (see global climate map, page 6) directly influences the different types of plant and animal that live there.

Your local ecosystems

A good way to get to know the ecology of your local area is to make a map of the areas of interest. Get hold of a large scale map of your district and copy the main features like roads and buildings, or photocopy it. Then go out and survey the area, noting down the position of important ecosystems. Fill these in on your map and make a key to explain the symbols and colours that you use. Once you have made your map, keep your eyes open for interesting things to add.

Example of an ecosystem map

Badger's set

Owl's nest

Key

	Woodland		Pond
	Hedgerow		Building
	River or stream		Road
†	Church		Graveyard
	Wheat-field		Meadow
	Bridge		Gate
×	Point of interest		Footpath

Food chains

The plants and animals in a given ecosystem are linked by their feeding relationships. The plants act as producers (see page 7) by using the sun's energy to produce food, which provides animals with the energy they need to live. The energy stored in plants as food is passed on through the community in a **food chain**. It is passed on directly to **primary consumers**, animals which eat plants, and indirectly to **secondary consumers**, animals which eat primary consumers. Other animals eat these secondary consumers and are known as **tertiary consumers**.

Each food chain also contains **decomposers**. These are bacteria, fungi and some types of insects that break down dead plant and animal matter into minerals and humus in the soil. In the process, they get their own energy for life from the food that they break down.

Decomposers at work

Find an old log and make a study of its decay. Take notes or photographs over a period of time of the different decomposers at work. How long does it take?

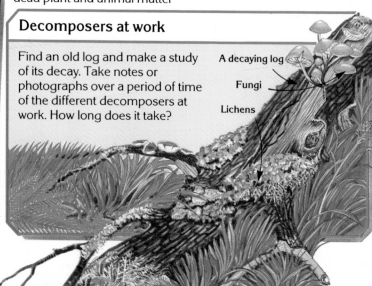

A decaying log

Fungi

Lichens

Food webs

Each ecosystem contains many different food chains which interlink to form a more complex **food web**. This is because animals often eat a varied diet and so play different roles in a number of food chains. Patterns of feeding also link different ecosystems. Animals from one will feed off plants and animals from another. In this way, all life on earth is interlinked in one vast, continuous web.

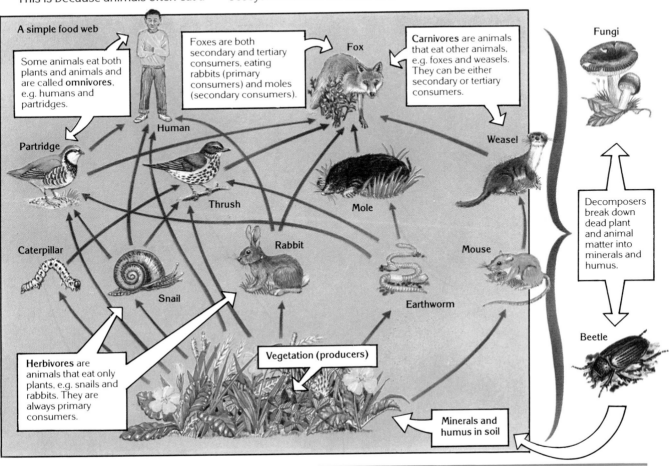

A simple food web

Some animals eat both plants and animals and are called **omnivores**, e.g. humans and partridges.

Foxes are both secondary and tertiary consumers, eating rabbits (primary consumers) and moles (secondary consumers).

Carnivores are animals that eat other animals, e.g. foxes and weasels. They can be either secondary or tertiary consumers.

Fungi

Decomposers break down dead plant and animal matter into minerals and humus.

Herbivores are animals that eat only plants, e.g. snails and rabbits. They are always primary consumers.

Vegetation (producers)

Minerals and humus in soil

Partridge · Human · Fox · Weasel · Thrush · Mole · Caterpillar · Snail · Rabbit · Earthworm · Mouse · Beetle

Constructing a food web

To show how complicated a food web can be, you can build your own. Find some old wildlife magazines, cut out pictures of individual plants and animals, and stick them onto some card. You could also trace, copy or draw them from books. Then arrange the pictures in a food web, connecting those that eat or are eaten by each other. Make different webs for different ecosystems, e.g. your local area, an African plain or the Amazon rainforest. The more pictures you find, the more complex the web will be.

String, yarn or ribbon linking pictures.

Trophic levels

Trophic levels are a way of looking at the levels in a food chain from the point of view of energy. At each level in the chain, some of the food taken in is broken down for energy and some is stored. This means that, for a given amount of food at the bottom, some is lost at each step up to a higher level, leaving less to be broken down for energy. So fewer animals can be supported at each level on that amount of food.

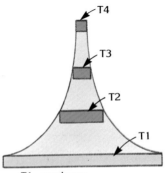

Pyramid of numbers
(number of individuals at each level)

T4
T3
T2
T1

T1 – producers
T2 – primary consumers
T3 – secondary consumers
T4 – tertiary consumers

The ocean

The oceans of the world form one vast ecosystem covering over 70% of the planet's surface. Many varied ecosystems exist within it, each with its own environment and diversity of life-forms. This vast area is little known, but it contains a wealth of resources. With more understanding and cooperation, its vast store of food, minerals and energy can be gained for the benefit of all.

These two views of the earth show the true extent of the enormous ocean ecosystem.

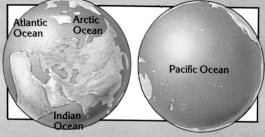

Atlantic Ocean

Arctic Ocean

Pacific Ocean

Indian Ocean

Marine habitats

The underwater landscape is just as varied as that on land, with countless different habitats and communities. There are vast areas of sandy desert, huge mountain ranges and areas rich in plant and animal life. The most spectacular of these are the tropical coral reefs. Despite existing only in relatively small areas of the vast oceans, they support a third of all fish species.

The marine food cycle

The ocean ecosystem has a vast and complicated food web (see page 9). From single-celled organisms to massive whales, the ocean is home to a range of plant and animal life that is just as diverse as that on land.

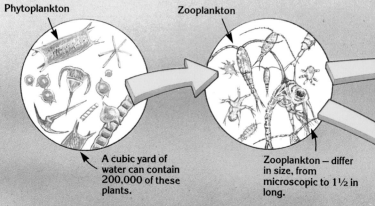

Phytoplankton

Zooplankton

A cubic yard of water can contain 200,000 of these plants.

Zooplankton – differ in size, from microscopic to 1½ in long.

Almost all of the ocean's varied plant and animal life exists in the top 325 ft where sunlight can penetrate. The ocean's producers, microscopic plants called **phytoplankton**, live very close to the surface as they need the sun's energy for the process of photosynthesis. Like green plants on land, these tiny marine plants provide the basis of all life in the oceans.

Using energy absorbed from the sun, phytoplankton combine water and carbon dioxide to produce carbohydrates, the basic elements of all food webs. In the process they produce almost 70% of the world's oxygen. Phytoplankton are consumed by microscopic animals called **zooplankton**. These and other tiny creatures are eaten in turn by small fish. And so on up the food chain.

The Great Barrier Reef is one of the natural wonders of the world. Up to 170 m (500 feet) across and stretching over 2,100 km (1,260 miles) along the north-east coast of Australia, it is home to over 3,000 animal species.

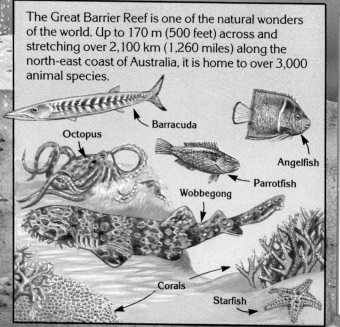

Barracuda

Octopus

Angelfish

Parrotfish

Wobbegong

Corals

Starfish

Studying plankton

If you get the chance, study a sample of seawater under a microscope. Or study water from a pond or stream – plankton live in freshwater too. The variety of life-forms is amazing. Can you find any of these common forms of plankton?

Phytoplankton:

Diatom

Silicoflagellate

Dinoflagellate

Zooplankton:

Crab larva

Arrowworm

Copepod

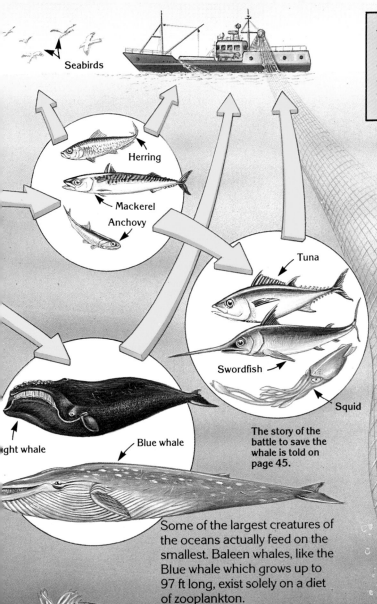

Seabirds

Herring

Mackerel

Anchovy

Tuna

Swordfish

Squid

The story of the battle to save the whale is told on page 45.

ght whale

Blue whale

Some of the largest creatures of the oceans actually feed on the smallest. Baleen whales, like the Blue whale which grows up to 97 ft long, exist solely on a diet of zooplankton.

Sea anemone

Swimming crab

Dead matter sinks to the ocean floor where it is either eaten by bottom dwellers (in shallower areas), like crabs and sea anemones, or it decays, producing minerals. Some form new rock, the rest are circulated by currents and taken in by plants.

The average depth of the ocean is 4050 yds, though parts are much deeper. Even the darkest depths are not devoid of life, however – thousands of weird and wonderful creatures have adapted to life in near total darkness.

Angler fish – creates its own light to attract the smaller fish which it feeds on.

The ocean itself plays a vital role in the earth's water cycle. Its huge surface area allows vast quantities of water to evaporate into the atmosphere. The water then condenses to form clouds (for more on the water cycle, see page 12).

Fishing

For thousands of years, man has harvested fish from the seas as a valuable food source. Today the global catch plays a vital part in feeding the world's growing population.

A fish diet?

How often do you eat fish? They are very good for you: high in protein and low in fat. Find out what sorts are available in your area, and where they come from. Have any become rarer or more expensive?

Over-fishing by large modern fishing fleets now threatens the livelihoods of traditional fishermen throughout the world. This has caused stocks of many fish species to become dangerously low. It is now vital that we have more international cooperation to sustain fish harvests.

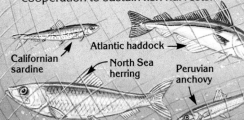

Californian sardine

North Sea herring

Atlantic haddock

Peruvian anchovy

These species have all suffered the effects of over-fishing.

Pollution

Pollution is now a major problem in marine ecosystems. Over 80% of this comes from land-based activities, e.g. sewage and industrial waste. Conditions are worst in enclosed areas like the Mediterranean and the North Sea, where levels of pollution are now so high that wildlife and human health are threatened. Measures are finally being taken to combat this international problem, but it will be a long and difficult job.

Drum containing dangerous radioactive nuclear waste dumped at sea.

Cycles in nature

All living things can be found within a relatively thin layer on or near the surface of the earth. Apart from the sun's energy, all their needs are supplied by the small proportion of the earth's resources contained in this layer. If the water, oxygen and other elements vital for life were only used once, they would soon run out. This is why many of nature's processes work in cycles. There is a constant exchange of the elements between air, earth, water, plants and animals, and these recycling processes ensure that all living things are able to live and grow.

One of the most important elements is oxygen, which exists freely as a gas in the atmosphere (21%), and is also an essential part of both the water and carbon cycles. Carbon itself and nitrogen are also vital. Others of importance include the minerals phosphorus, sulphur and calcium, and trace elements, like iron and zinc, that are needed in smaller quantities. These are all needed to supply energy for life, and are also important in the process of growth and constant renewal of all living cells.

The water cycle

Water is an essential of life, making up almost 75% of all living things. It is continuously recycled between sea, air and land, creating the conditions in which life can exist.

Make your own water cycle

Using a large plastic bowl, a small container and some plastic wrap, you can make a miniature water cycle. Leave the bowl in the sun, with some water in it. The heat evaporates the water, which rises and condenses on the cool plastic to fall into the container.

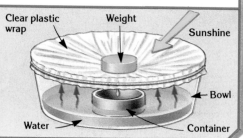

Clear plastic wrap — Weight — Sunshine — Bowl — Water — Container

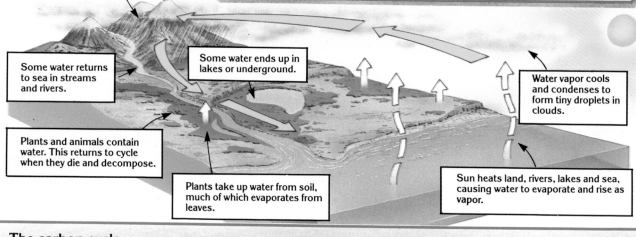

Clouds meet cold air, e.g. above mountains. Large drops of water form and fall as rain or snow.

Some water returns to sea in streams and rivers.

Some water ends up in lakes or underground.

Water vapor cools and condenses to form tiny droplets in clouds.

Plants and animals contain water. This returns to cycle when they die and decompose.

Plants take up water from soil, much of which evaporates from leaves.

Sun heats land, rivers, lakes and sea, causing water to evaporate and rise as vapor.

The carbon cycle

Carbon is constantly circulating in many different forms through living things, the soil and the atmosphere.

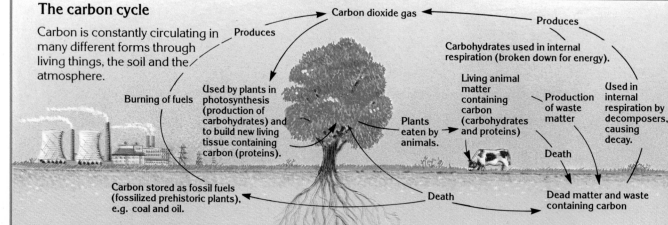

Carbon dioxide gas

Produces

Produces

Carbohydrates used in internal respiration (broken down for energy).

Burning of fuels

Used by plants in photosynthesis (production of carbohydrates) and to build new living tissue containing carbon (proteins).

Plants eaten by animals.

Living animal matter containing carbon (carbohydrates and proteins)

Production of waste matter

Used in internal respiration by decomposers, causing decay.

Death

Carbon stored as fossil fuels (fossilized prehistoric plants), e.g. coal and oil.

Death

Dead matter and waste containing carbon

The greenhouse effect

Carbon dioxide in the atmosphere plays an important role in warming the earth by trapping the sun's heat, in what is called the greenhouse effect. Since industrialization, the burning of fossil fuels has greatly increased the amount of carbon dioxide in the atmosphere.

The future effects of this build-up on global temperatures can only be guessed at. Some experts predict that temperatures will rise, melting the polar ice packs, raising sea levels to flood coastal areas, and resulting in large-scale changes in climate and agriculture around the world.

To keep the level of carbon dioxide from rising further we must increase our use of renewable energy sources and become more energy-efficient (see page 33).

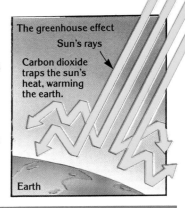

The greenhouse effect
Sun's rays
Carbon dioxide traps the sun's heat, warming the earth.
Earth

The nitrogen cycle

All living things need nitrogen to build proteins for growth. The way they get this is quite complex.

Although about 78% of air is made up of the gas nitrogen, it cannot be used by plants and animals in gaseous form. It must first be converted into nitrites and then nitrates before it can be used.

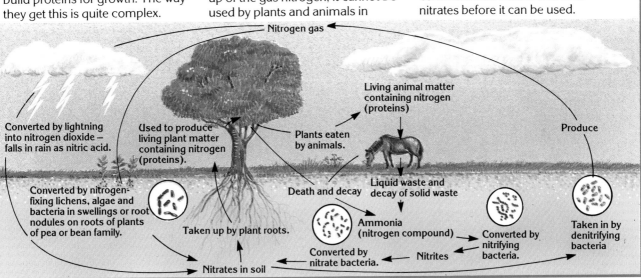

Nitrogen gas

Living animal matter containing nitrogen (proteins)

Produce

Converted by lightning into nitrogen dioxide — falls in rain as nitric acid.

Used to produce living plant matter containing nitrogen (proteins).

Plants eaten by animals.

Converted by nitrogen-fixing lichens, algae and bacteria in swellings or root nodules on roots of plants of pea or bean family.

Taken up by plant roots.

Death and decay

Liquid waste and decay of solid waste

Ammonia (nitrogen compound)

Converted by nitrifying bacteria.

Taken in by denitrifying bacteria

Nitrates in soil

Converted by nitrate bacteria.

Nitrites

The mineral cycle

Minerals originate from the earth itself, either from the surface or from deeper down through volcanic activity. Many of these, like phosphorus and iron, are needed for the life processes of plants and animals.

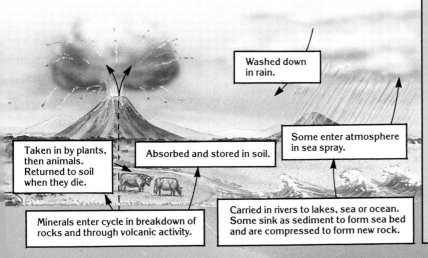

Washed down in rain.

Some enter atmosphere in sea spray.

Taken in by plants, then animals. Returned to soil when they die.

Absorbed and stored in soil.

Minerals enter cycle in breakdown of rocks and through volcanic activity.

Carried in rivers to lakes, sea or ocean. Some sink as sediment to form sea bed and are compressed to form new rock.

The natural balance

Nature's cycles are relatively stable. Any changes that do occur take place within certain limits, so that, despite minor variations, the cycles continue and life goes on. However, man's activities are fundamentally changing the environment and disturbing these natural cycles. We are upsetting the fine balance of nature, and the results may turn out to be disastrous.

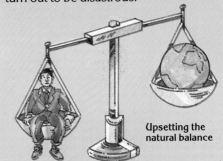

Upsetting the natural balance

Disturbing the cycles

Nature's cycles form a balance in the natural world in which there is no waste. Everything is broken down and re-used. Man, however, is now creating an imbalance by creating waste and polluting the environment. Pollution occurs on different levels: personal, national and global.

Pollution

Ever since people first gathered together in settlements there has been pollution. This describes everything produced by man that does not decompose (is not **biodegradable**) and so does not return into the natural cycles. It also describes our disturbance of these cycles by producing more or less of a natural substance and so upsetting the balance.

Some pollution just looks bad, whilst other forms, like some chemical and nuclear wastes, are deadly. When population was low and there was little industry, a small amount of pollution did not really matter. Nowadays, things are very different.

An early rubbish tip
A modern tip

Recycling waste

Unlike nature, modern man produces vast amounts of waste. The average family of four in an industrialized country throws away over a ton of garbage a year, most of which ends up buried below ground. But how much of this actually is garbage.

Step 1

Study the contents of your garbage can to see what you are throwing away (do it outside on newspaper). Weigh the contents and separate them, putting them into different containers, e.g. glass, food waste, plastics, textiles, paper and metals.

You should have your parents' permission (or help) before doing this.

Wear a pair of washing-up gloves and overalls or old clothes.

Never taste or inhale unknown substances.

Be very careful of broken glass and the sharp edges of tin cans.

Step 2

Now see how much can be returned into nature's cycles or recycled for human use. Here are a few examples of how this can be done – for more ideas, contact your local environmental or conservation group (see pages 44-45).

Glass. There may well be a glass-recycling scheme in your area, in which you take your bottles and jars to bottle-banks. Ask your local authority about this. Or you can invent ways of re-using jars and bottles, e.g. as containers or vases.

Using a bottle bank

Paper. Many charities and organizations collect bundles of old newspapers and magazines to be recycled. Contact those in your area, e.g. an old people's home, to see if you and your friends can help. To make your own recycled paper, see pages 42-43.

Aluminum cans. These can be washed, crushed (stand on them) and taken to a can recycling center (look in the phone book). You may be paid for them. You could collect more at concerts, fairs, fetes, etc.

Only aluminum cans can be recycled. Use a magnet to check.

Aluminum cans are not magnetic, other cans are.

Organic waste. This is anything that will rot. It can be used as compost (see page 38).

Step 3

What is left, like plastics and chemicals, cannot at the moment be recycled. Weigh this waste – the less there is the better. See if you can decrease your family's waste, e.g. by buying products with less packaging, or by always taking the same bag to the shops with you.

Acid rain

One of the nastiest forms of pollution that we are creating today is known as acid rain. This occurs when wastes from burning fossil fuels interfere with the natural water cycle. Its effects include dying forests, lifeless lakes, damaged buildings and harm to people. We have the technology to prevent this happening, e.g. filters for power stations and catalytic converters to clean fumes from vehicle exhaust pipes. Some countries have already begun using such measures in an attempt to stop acid rain. Others have been much slower to see that action is now vital.

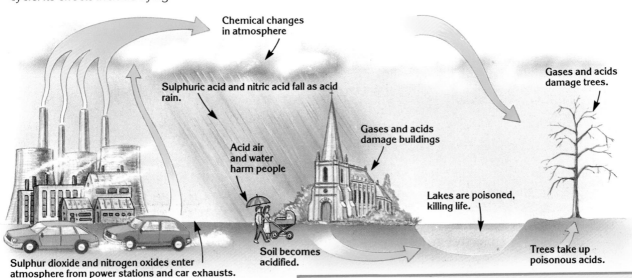

Chemical changes in atmosphere

Sulphuric acid and nitric acid fall as acid rain.

Acid air and water harm people

Gases and acids damage buildings

Gases and acids damage trees.

Lakes are poisoned, killing life.

Trees take up poisonous acids.

Soil becomes acidified.

Sulphur dioxide and nitrogen oxides enter atmosphere from power stations and car exhausts.

Chemicals in farming

In today's intensive farming the natural nitrogen and mineral cycles are neglected. Very little natural organic waste is returned to the soil, resulting in reduced levels of minerals and humus, and lower productivity. To make up for this, farmers add chemical fertilizers to the soil. These often cause environmental and health damage, e.g. when washed into rivers and lakes, eventually ending up in drinking water.

Intensive farming in Montana, USA

Many powerful chemicals are also used to fight pests, weeds and diseases in order to keep productivity high. These pesticides, herbicides and fungicides have long-lasting and damaging effects on food webs wherever they are used. The chemicals often remain on the plants which have been sprayed, and can damage human health when these are eaten.

Organic farming

Fuel shortages, increasing costs and environmental damage mean the long-term future of intensive farming is in doubt. We need to return to more natural farming methods, which work with nature's cycles. These methods are based on ecological principles and are known as organic farming.

Organic farming techniques, like crop rotation and the use of manure as fertilizer, are today being used successfully. They improve rather than endanger the environment by returning most organic waste to the soil, increasing humus and mineral levels and allowing nature's cycles to work.

Crop rotation
Some crops use up the nitrates in the soil and others (beans and peas) restore them (see page 13). By changing the crop grown in a field each year in a rota system, the natural cycles can be used to improve growth.

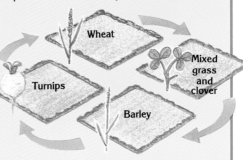

Wheat

Mixed grass and clover

Turnips

Barley

Ecologists think that these techniques should be widely adopted. Many people now prefer to eat "organic" food, knowing that it is free of chemicals and has been produced without damaging the environment.

Adaptation

All living things must adapt to their environment if they are going to survive. Adaptation is the result of long-term interaction with the environment and has enabled life to spread to every part of the world. It includes changes in both behavior and physical features.

Hot deserts

Some of the best examples of adaptation occur in the world's deserts (large areas with extremely harsh environments). In hot, dry desert climates, plants and animals have developed various different survival techniques, e.g. many have physical adaptations to store water or food, or to lose heat more rapidly.

The Australian outback is the largest area of sandy desert outside the Sahara. It is made up of different types of desert, varying due to differences in climate and rock formation. The first inhabitants of the land, the Aborigines, developed a lifestyle over many thousands of years which enabled them to live in both grassland and desert. Until very recently, groups still wandered the outback, hunting and gathering food in their traditional ways.

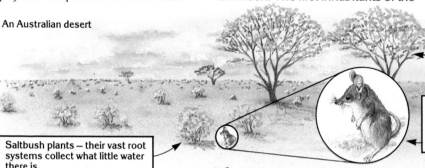

An Australian desert

Mulga trees — they have expanded leaf stalks instead of leaves to lessen water loss by evaporation.

Marsupial mice — they avoid the day's heat in burrows and search for food at night. Their tails store fat reserves in case of food shortages.

Saltbush plants — their vast root systems collect what little water there is.

There are many other examples of adaptations to life in hot deserts. Cacti, for example, have developed spines instead of leaves to prevent water loss, and the North American jack rabbit has developed very large ears (see picture).

North American jack rabbit

The long ears contain many blood vessels near the surface, which radiate away the body's heat.

Desertification

This is when dry, marginal land is turned into desert due to human activities like over-grazing or cutting down trees. Much of the earth's land surface is now threatened. The costs of preventing this and improving the damaged lands are low when compared to the gains in agricultural production once the lands are developed. But at present very little is being done and many traditional farmers, with little land or stock, are suffering badly.

The Sahel, Africa: early 1970s

Drought and desertification changed marginal land (land that is difficult to cultivate) into desert.

Over 100,000 people and millions of animals died.

Growing a cactus garden

A shallow clay container filled with sandy soil and decorated with some stones or wood is all you need as a basis for your cactus garden. To obtain your cacti either buy them or take cuttings from someone else's plants. To do this, break off the shoots growing at the base of the parent cactus. Let them dry for a few days before putting them in the soil. Once established, cacti need a lot of sun but very little watering or attention.

A cactus garden

If you dribble water onto cacti, it will roll off. Their "skin" does not allow water to be lost, so it can't get in either.

Hedge cactus (Cereus)

Old man cactus (Cephalocereus)

Fig cactus (Opuntia)

Golden ball (Echinocactus)

Icy deserts

Conditions in the freezing, icy deserts of the polar regions are just as harsh as in their hot, dry equivalents. In winter, ice and snow cover the vast continent of Antarctica and its surrounding seas, as well as the entire Arctic region (see below). But living things can still be found, adapted to life in these extreme environments.

Polar bears survive the winter by hibernating in dens hollowed out under the ice. They also have large, furry feet to act as snowshoes.

Arctic fox — the color of its coat changes to fit the season: pure white in winter, browny-red in summer. This is an example of camouflage (see below).

To survive the cold, all the large animals are warm-blooded, that is, able to keep their body temperature constant despite external conditions. Thick, insulating layers of fat or fur, or both, keep the heat in and the cold out.

Huskies curl into balls to conserve heat and are protected by their thick coats of fur.

The native Eskimo people face the cold by smearing themselves with animal fat and wearing thick furs.

The Arctic summer

In the brief summers much of the ice and snow melts, revealing the Arctic tundra, which, for a while, supports a great variety of plant and animal life. The plants survive the long winter either as seeds or by not freezing (many contain "anti-freeze"), and grow and produce seeds in the short summer. Hot, dry deserts, too, have short periods when life is plentiful. These occur after rain, when water brings life to dormant seeds.

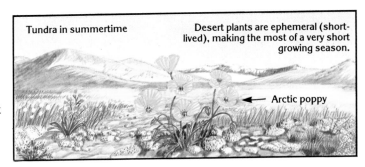

Tundra in summertime

Desert plants are ephemeral (short-lived), making the most of a very short growing season.

Arctic poppy

Camouflage and mimicry

Camouflage is the adaptation of a plant or animal to blend in with its natural surroundings so as not to be seen. This adaptation has developed to help plants and animals hide from predators. But it is also used by predators themselves to remain unseen by unsuspecting prey. Mimicry is a camouflage technique, by which animals have adapted to look like, or mimic, something else, so as to benefit in a particular way.

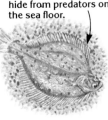

Plaice — uses its dull, sandy coloration to hide from predators on the sea floor.

Bee-orchid — its flower looks like a bee. This attracts bees looking for a mate, which then pollinate the plant.

A seed study

Not only do plants adapt to the environment around them, but their seeds do, too, giving them a greater chance to survive. In many cases, they are adapted for wind dispersal. Collect as many different seeds as you can find and compare the variety of shapes and sizes. Take them outside, throw them into the air and study how, and how far, they travel.

Seed adaptations

Feathery seeds, e.g. dandelion

Explosive fruits (launch seed away from plant), e.g. gorse

Seed in edible fruit (dispersed in droppings of animal that eats it), e.g. bramble

Helicopter seeds, e.g. maple or sycamore

Coniferous and deciduous forests

Coniferous and deciduous forests are two of the three major types of forest (see also tropical rainforest, pages 26-27). Life in the two areas has developed very differently, due to the differences in climate, as the examples on these pages show.

Man and the forests

Man's influence on the world's forests is wide-ranging. Forestry is very important to the economies of many countries, supplying wood to the paper, building and furniture industries, but it can often be ecologically damaging.

This is especially true when plantation trees of different, fast-growing species are planted to replace native trees – destroying wildlife habitats, endangering species, and ruining landscapes.

A coniferous plantation

Plantations are important sources of wood, but can be ecologically damaging.

Very little of the great deciduous and mixed forests of the past survive today, due to the spread of farming and urban developments.

Man's destructive activities, like the production of acid rain (see page 15), now threaten those that remain. We must realize the dangers and act now to protect these trees. To find out how to choose, plant and care for a tree, see pages 40-41.

Coniferous forests

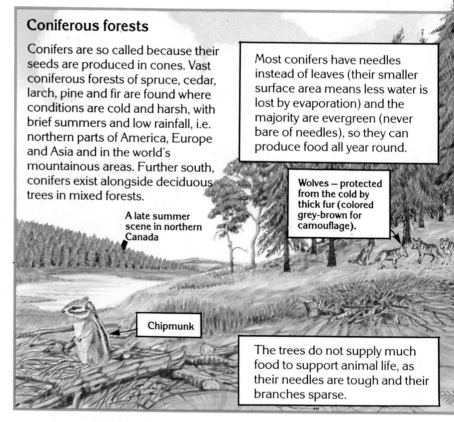

Conifers are so called because their seeds are produced in cones. Vast coniferous forests of spruce, cedar, larch, pine and fir are found where conditions are cold and harsh, with brief summers and low rainfall, i.e. northern parts of America, Europe and Asia and in the world's mountainous areas. Further south, conifers exist alongside deciduous trees in mixed forests.

A late summer scene in northern Canada

Most conifers have needles instead of leaves (their smaller surface area means less water is lost by evaporation) and the majority are evergreen (never bare of needles), so they can produce food all year round.

Wolves – protected from the cold by thick fur (colored grey-brown for camouflage).

Chipmunk

The trees do not supply much food to support animal life, as their needles are tough and their branches sparse.

Deciduous forests

The word deciduous describes trees that shed their leaves once a year. They are flowering plants, mainly blooming once a year in the spring. Deciduous forests are found in areas with relatively mild temperatures and plenty of rainfall throughout the year. Most of Europe, Japan, eastern Asia and the eastern USA were once covered in forests of deciduous trees, like oak, beech, maple and ash.

A summer scene in the eastern USA

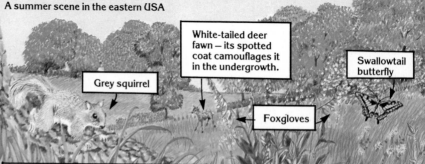

White-tailed deer fawn – its spotted coat camouflages it in the undergrowth.

Grey squirrel

Swallowtail butterfly

Foxgloves

Deciduous trees have large, broad leaves to make the most of the many months of sunshine for photosynthesis. They are lost before winter when strong winds and cold would damage them.

Each tree provides homes and food for a large wildlife community. Rich soil and plenty of sunshine allow many different plants to flourish. These support still more animal life.

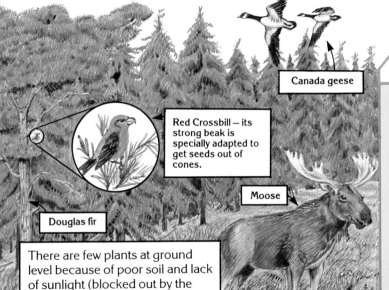

Canada geese

Red Crossbill — its strong beak is specially adapted to get seeds out of cones.

Moose

Douglas fir

There are few plants at ground level because of poor soil and lack of sunlight (blocked out by the conifers). This limits animal life throughout the forest.

It is too cold for most bacteria and earthworms, so decomposition of plant matter is slow, the soil remains in undisturbed layers and there is little humus. This results in less effective nitrogen and mineral cycles.

Some animals have adapted to life in the forest all year round, e.g. moose wander far to find food, and bears and chipmunks hibernate in winter, living off fat stored from summer food.

The brief warm summer sees much more activity. Insects multiply rapidly, supplying food, e.g. for birds flocking north to nest. The conifers grow fast to make the most of the extra sun.

Identifying conifers

The shape of a conifer's needles will tell you which group of trees it belongs to. These are the major groups:

Larches: clusters of 12-20 short needles, fall in autumn.

Pines: two or more needles, joined at base.

Firs: individual needles with blunt tips.

Spruces: pointed, stiff and four-sided needles.

Cedars and junipers: small, flat, scale-shaped leaves.

Yews: flattened, leathery needles.

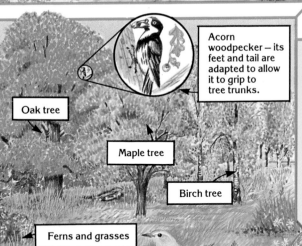

Acorn woodpecker — its feet and tail are adapted to allow it to grip to tree trunks.

Oak tree

Maple tree

Birch tree

Ferns and grasses

Yellow warbler

Pigmy shrew

A yearly fall of leaves and an abundance of decomposers create a soil which is rich in humus, nitrates and minerals.

Animal activity in winter is greater than in coniferous forests, but life is still more plentiful in the warm, sunny conditions of spring and summer. Plant life, insects, birds and mammals are abundant.

Measuring tree heights

Pin a strip of paper to the tree at your height and measure this (in inches). Walk away from the tree, holding a ruler at arms length, until the strip is level with the 1 in mark (see picture). Note where the tree-top reaches on the in scale and multiply by your height (e.g. 10 in times 57 in = 570 in or 47½ ft.)

Your view from the right distance

Read off in scale here.

Large ruler

Mark on tree is at 1 in mark on ruler.

0 in on ruler should be level with bottom of tree.

In southern Europe, the south-west USA, Australia, New Zealand and southern South America, many deciduous trees have adapted to very hot, dry summers by adopting coniferous features. They are evergreen, with smaller, thicker leaves to save water.

Relationships in nature

In the natural world, many of the relationships between living things (organisms) are to do with eating or being eaten, but there are just as many in which organisms work together, often to the advantage of those involved. There are many different ways in which this happens, some simple, others complex; some examples are given on these pages.

Living together

Many plants and animals live with others of the same species in groups of differing sizes, with different degrees of interaction. Small numbers of animals living together are known as social groups. Larger gatherings are known as colonies.

Lions, for example, live in small social groups called prides, in which the females do the hunting as well as caring for the young. In many social groups, however, there is a more equal sharing of the work, e.g. African meerkats (small desert mammals) take turns to look after the group's offspring. The large apes come closest to our own social grouping, with the young brought up in a family framework.

A group of rare mountain gorillas — inhabitants of the upper reaches of the rainforests of Zaire.

Colonies

Different colonial animals show different levels of social behaviour, and the degree of dependence between individuals differs greatly. Many seabirds, like gannets and penguins, only form colonies out of mutual self-interest (for safety in numbers).

A colony of cormorants

Seabird colonies can be enormous — one Peruvian island was at one point home to about 5 million cormorants.

Other creatures, however, like ants, termites and bees, live together in far more complex colonies, with groups of related individuals playing specific roles (examples are given in "keeping an ant colony", above right). They depend on each other for the smooth running and continuation of the colony.

Keeping an ant colony

Ants are easy to keep and fascinating to watch. To see how to make an ant observatory, properly called a formicarium, like the one illustrated, turn to page 36. You can watch the ants at work within it and study their social behaviour without disturbing them too much.

An ant observatory

Look for ants playing different roles: guarding the colony, finding food, tending the young, and looking after the queen.

Watch the ants construct a complex system of passageways and chambers.

Study which foods the ants prefer, by leaving them different sorts.

Study the different stages of their life cycle and the role of the queen.

Super-organisms

The word super-organism describes the closest form of colonial relationship, in which single organisms work together so closely that they effectively form a larger structure with its own, self-contained existence.

Coral is an example of this. Thousands of tiny animals called polyps combine to form a much larger coral structure. These polyps are interconnected by a network of links through which food can be shared.

Another example is the Portuguese man-of-war. This is not in fact a jellyfish, but a colony of many specialized polyps, each fulfilling a specific task. The resulting super-organism is a more effective life-form than the individual animals it is made up of.

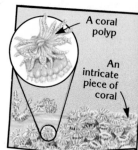

A coral polyp

An intricate piece of coral

A Portuguese man-of-war

Symbiosis

Symbiosis describes the very close relationship between two organisms of different species that live together and gain from their interaction. One common example of this is lichen, which is found on stone and wood surfaces. The main part of a lichen's body is a fungus, within which live one or more tiny, single-celled plants called algae. Both benefit greatly from their mutual arrangement (see right).

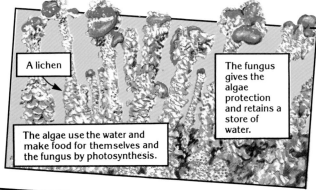

A lichen

The fungus gives the algae protection and retains a store of water.

The algae use the water and make food for themselves and the fungus by photosynthesis.

Here are two more examples of symbiosis:

In Africa ox-peckers eat insects that irritate antelope.

They also give warning of danger by flying up noisily.

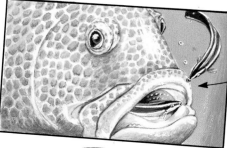

This large fish allows the smaller fish to feed on parasites that live in its mouth.

Commensalism

Literally "eating at the same table", commensalism describes a relationship (less close than in symbiosis) between two organisms of different species in which food is involved. In most cases, one partner takes advantage of the feeding habits of another and gives little or nothing in return. The relationship between the house mouse and humans is a good example of commensalism.

The mouse takes advantage of food left around the house.

Humans gain nothing from the relationship.

Co-operation

There are many other forms of co-operation between living things in nature, in which both participants benefit in some way, like plants needing insects for pollination and so attracting them with nectar.

Parasites

Not all close relationships are beneficial. A parasite is a plant or animal that lives on or in another organism (the host), taking food from it while giving nothing or actually harming it in return. A parasite will rarely kill its host, though, as this would result in its own death, too. Lice and fleas are common parasites. Humans are often hosts to these and many others, like tapeworm and roundworm, and they also suffer from diseases, like malaria, carried by parasites.

Tapeworms up to 12½ ft long can sometimes be found in the human intestine.

Investigating plant galls

Plant galls are home to the larvae of various insects, which are parasitic on certain trees. The adults lay their eggs inside a leaf or bud, which reacts to this intrusion by forming a growth around them. The egg turns into the larva within the gall, later emerging as an adult insect.

Plant galls can be found on many plants and trees (especially oak, birch and willow) in spring and early summer. Go out and collect some, bringing back the leaves they are on. Place them in a jar with holes in its lid, keeping this outside, and watch for the adult insect to emerge.

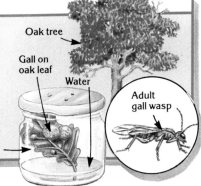

Oak tree

Gall on oak leaf

Water

Adult gall wasp

Glass jar

Population and conservation

In the natural world there is a fragile balance in plant and animal populations. There are several ways that their numbers are naturally kept in check, some of which are dealt with on this page. However, this is no longer true of the human population, the growth of which is fast destroying nature's balance, with alarming consequences for our planet.

Population control

A relatively stable balance of numbers is maintained in the wild through competition and co-existence. Predator/prey relationships and territorial behavior are the main reasons of achieving this, and these are well illustrated by the wildlife of the African savannah (see below).

Territorial behavior

All living things need food, shelter and living space. As a means of gaining these, many animals behave territorially – that is, they live (as individuals or as a social group) in a defined space, or territory, which is large enough to cater for their needs. This territory is defended against others of the same species, with the result that the overall population is kept down.

The niche

The role of an animal in its community, including what it eats, where it lives and its position in the food chain is known as its ecological niche. Different species cannot live in the same niche – they compete for resources and living space until one is forced out. Sometimes it appears that two animals share the same niche, but a closer look will show that they inhabit separate, though overlapping, ones.

> Elephants feed on tall grass, while buffalo eat the young shoots and antelope graze on the short grass that is left — each occupies a different niche.

> African buffalo — each herd keeps to a territory several miles wide.

Predators

Predators are animals that catch and eat other animals. They play a vital role in every ecosystem, by keeping down the population of herbivores and smaller predators on which they feed.

> A pride of lions — feed on the many grazing animals, like zebra and wildebeest. Each pride has a territory of up to 5 miles across.

Feeding birds

Bird feeders or a bird table will encourage a variety of bird life into your garden or to your windowsill. Watch their different feeding preferences and techniques to work out the different niches they occupy. For details on how to make a bird table, see page 39.

Experiment with various types of food, like nuts, seeds or meat, to see what different birds prefer.

Feeding the birds throughout the winter could keep them alive.

Experiment with different feeders, like hanging bags of nuts or half a coconut, to see the birds' different feeding techniques.

Watching predators

Try to study the predators that can be found around you. Watch the domestic cat stalking its prey — it often demonstrates the hunting techniques of its much larger African relatives. Other common predators worth studying are the birds of prey (known as raptors), like hawks and kestrels.

A kestrel watching its prey (small mammals).

Smaller birds of prey often hunt beside roads and in open country.

The population problem

The world's human population is now over five billion and is rising rapidly (for more on the population problem, see page 32). This sheer weight of numbers, combined with the growing destruction caused by man, is putting great pressure on the world's wildlife and habitats. It is estimated that one plant or animal species becomes extinct every half an hour, while once common natural habitats are rapidly disappearing.

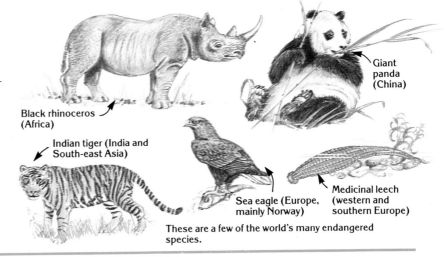

Black rhinoceros (Africa)

Giant panda (China)

Indian tiger (India and South-east Asia)

Sea eagle (Europe, mainly Norway)

Medicinal leech (western and southern Europe)

These are a few of the world's many endangered species.

Threatened habitats and wildlife

Urban expansion and the spread of intensive industry, agriculture and forestry are resulting in the destruction of important natural habitats. When these disappear, so do the many wild plants and animals that depend on them. For example, vital marine habitats, like saltmarshes and mangroves, are being polluted and destroyed at an alarming rate.

Mangrove swamp

Result of mangrove destruction

Man's greed for exotic luxuries, like fur coats and ivory jewelry, has meant that millions of animals are killed every year. As well as this, many more are caught to supply zoos, the pet trade and industrial and medical research centers. Many animals, like the cheetah and the polar bear, are now seriously endangered. This world-wide trade in wild animals is often illegal and always causes great suffering.

The need for conservation

Protection, or conservation, of wildlife and habitats is now more important than ever. The international agreements we have at present are too often ignored. We need to protect endangered species and habitats much more carefully. But in the end, it is only by becoming more aware of how we all affect the earth's environment that we will be able to safeguard the natural world.

The giant panda is the emblem of the World Wide Fund for Nature (formerly the World Wildlife Fund).

Since 1961, they have campaigned to protect the world's habitats and wildlife.

For more on what they and other organizations are doing, see pages 44-45.

Helping endangered wildlife

In every country of the world there are endangered plants and animals. Find out what is threatened in yours by contacting conservation or environmental groups (see pages 44-45). You could help them in their campaigns to help these species, or you could perhaps start your own group (see pages 42-43) to make local people more aware of the problems.

Another way to help these species is to protect or create the habitats that they prefer. Building a pond (see pages 5 and 36-37) and creating a pocket park (see pages 25 and 42-43) are two ways of doing this. Meadows, too, are easy to create, and are vital habitats for many

insects and rare wild flowers. If you have a garden, just leave an area of grass uncut and it will naturally develop into a meadow. If you live near a park, try to get the authorities to set aside an area as a meadow nature reserve.

A meadow reserve in a city park

23

Urban ecosystems

Surprising as it may seem, large towns and cities contain a great deal of wildlife. Wherever plants and animals can find suitable conditions, including enough food, warmth and shelter, they will move in. Many have adapted their ways to life amongst people in an urban environment.

Urban adaptations

The growth of towns and cities has produced similar urban environments all over the world. In different places, different animals have adapted to fill similar niches. For instance, the brush-tailed opossum, the raccoon and the red fox play the same kind of role in urban environments on their different continents. All originally lived in open woodland, but they adapted to farmland and urban areas when these took its place.

The brush-tailed opossum and the raccoon often live in the roof spaces of suburban houses, while the fox makes its den in parks and areas of wasteland. All three often scavenge in dustbins for scraps of food. Their ability to adapt to different habitats and their varied diet have enabled them to live successfully in man-made environments.

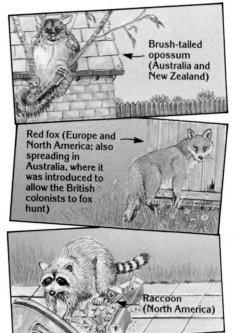

Brush-tailed opossum (Australia and New Zealand)

Red fox (Europe and North America; also spreading in Australia, where it was introduced to allow the British colonists to fox hunt)

Raccoon (North America)

One bird that is found only in man-made environments is the house sparrow. Originally feeding on grain, its diet is now far more varied. This, and its ability to nest on houses and other buildings, enables it to thrive in towns and cities.

House sparrow – spread across the world in the wake of the European colonizers.

Now common in Europe, North and South America, South Africa, Australia and New Zealand.

Succession

Wherever there is an area of abandoned land, it will not be long before nature moves in. Over a period of time, a variety of plants and animals will replace each other in a process called **succession**. Mosses and grasses will usually be the first arrivals, followed by flowering plants. These attract insects, which bring birds and other wild animals. If the land is left long enough, larger plants and trees will grow. See page 28 for more about succession.

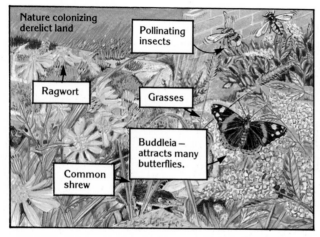

Nature colonizing derelict land

Pollinating insects

Ragwort

Grasses

Buddleia – attracts many butterflies.

Common shrew

City safari

You do not have to be in a tropical jungle or on an African plain to go on safari – a wildlife expedition around town can be just as rewarding. Study the plants and animals in those areas of your town or city that are slightly off the beaten track: wasteland, cemeteries, the wilder parts of the park and the riverbanks and canals. All you need for a satisfying safari is good observation, and perhaps a little patience. You could take your friends and make it a full-scale expedition.

Use a notebook for descriptions or sketches of what you see.

A good reference book is useful for identification.

Plan your safari before you set out, using a map of your town or city to find the areas which may be of most interest.

Transport and pollution

Pollution from the ever-growing volume of vehicle exhaust is making life more and more unpleasant in many of the world's major cities. The air contains many harmful gases like ozone, which is formed when nitrogen oxides from the exhaust react in sunlight with oxygen. Ozone, carbon monoxide, hydrocarbons and lead and dust particles all endanger the health of the cities' people and wildlife.

The removal of lead from gasoline and the use of devices known as three-way catalytic converters to control exhaust fumes are two ways of lessening the problem. A long term solution, however, will only come from radical changes in

In Tokyo, Japan, special electronic signs show the levels of noise and air pollution.

transport policy and city planning. A greater emphasis on improved rail systems and public transport, combined with methods of "traffic calming", will help achieve this.

An example of "traffic calming"

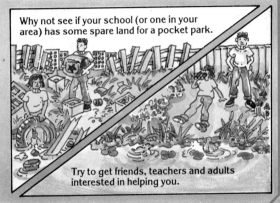

The aim is to create a better sense of community, safer roads and a pleasanter environment.

Pedestrians and cyclists are better catered for, with wider pavements and cycle paths.

Bends, bollards and road humps keep vehicle speed down.

The streets are made more attractive with trees, flowerbeds and benches.

A lichen pollution test

Plants called lichens are sensitive to air pollution, especially the air's acidity (see acid rain, page 15), so you can use their presence or absence to see how clean your air is. Shrubby and leafy lichens only survive in clean air. In the most polluted areas there are none at all. Look for lichens on walls, stones and trees, and use this scale to rate the air quality.

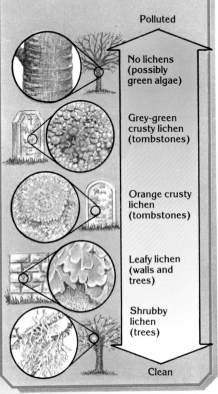

Polluted

No lichens (possibly green algae)

Grey-green crusty lichen (tombstones)

Orange crusty lichen (tombstones)

Leafy lichen (walls and trees)

Shrubby lichen (trees)

Clean

Creating a pocket park

Creating a miniature nature reserve, or pocket park, on derelict ground or wasteland is quite a task and probably calls for a team effort. The aim is to create a complete ecosystem in miniature, with perhaps a pond, areas of grassland and trees and bushes, in the heart of a town or city. It will provide pleasure for all the local people, and attract native wildlife back to the area.

There may already be a project in action in your area – ask at your local library, community center, or contact your local conservation or environmental group. You could probably join in and help. If not, you could search for a suitable site in your area (like a piece of wasteland) and start your own project with a group of friends (for more about this, see pages 42-43).

Why not see if your school (or one in your area) has some spare land for a pocket park.

Try to get friends, teachers and adults interested in helping you.

Tropical rainforests

Great rainforests stretch around the Equator, covering large parts of Central and South America, Central Africa, South-east Asia and northern Australasia. These forests are the most complex ecosystems in the world and contain a wealth of resources. Despite their importance, though, they are being destroyed at an alarming rate.

Rainforests grow in areas where rainfall and temperatures are both high and constant. Over millions of years they have developed into the earth's richest wildlife habitats. They cover less than 10% of the planet's land surface, but they contain between 50% and 70% of all plant and animal species. The greatest of all the forests is Amazonia in Brazil, featured on these pages.

Harpy eagle

Emerald tree boa

Toucan — its large, strong beak helps it pick fruit from a distance and also frightens predators.

Layering

All rain forests have a similar structure, with five main layers, each with its own specific plant and animal life. These layers often merge together, or sometimes one or more are absent.

Emergent layer — made up of a few of the tallest trees which rise 30 to 50 ft above the mass of greenery below. From here, Harpy eagles and other birds of prey watch alertly for the animals on which they feed.

Canopy — 100 to 130 ft above the ground, and some 30 ft thick, this is a continuous green roof formed by the interlinking leaves and branches of the tree tops. Most of the forest's many plants and animals are found here, taking advantage of the abundant sunshine.

Woolly monkey

Understorey — made up of the tops of smaller trees that receive less light, like palms, and of younger trees struggling to reach upwards. Much sparser than the canopy, it has its own community of plant and animal life.

Shrub layer — consisting of shrubs and small trees, this layer depends on sunlight penetrating the upper layers. If none reaches here, both this and the herb layer will be sparse.

When a gap appears in the canopy, sunlight reaches the lower regions, causing the shrub and herb layers to grow rapidly.

Herb layer — ferns and herbs making up a layer of undergrowth. Elusive ground dwellers, like the tapir, live down here, along with many insects.

Build your own rainforest

Using a large fish-tank, you can (almost) re-create the rainforest environment in miniature. Place a layer of gravel and charcoal at the bottom, covered with about an inch of rich compost. Shape the ground with small stones under the compost. Dampen the compost and add a variety of exotic plants.
With a glass top and kept in a warm, well-lit spot, out of the sun, the plants should flourish.

The air is moist, and water is continually recycled between compost, plant, air and tank. Add a little water every few months.

A variety of exotic plants — available from plant or flower shops.

Small flowering plants, like orchids, add color.

Delicate ferns

Don't plant them too close together, as they need room to grow.

Native Indian, hunting with blow-pipe. Brazil's Indian population has fallen from 5 million to 200,000 over the past 400 years.

Many of the largest trees have developed buttresses for support, as their roots are very shallow.

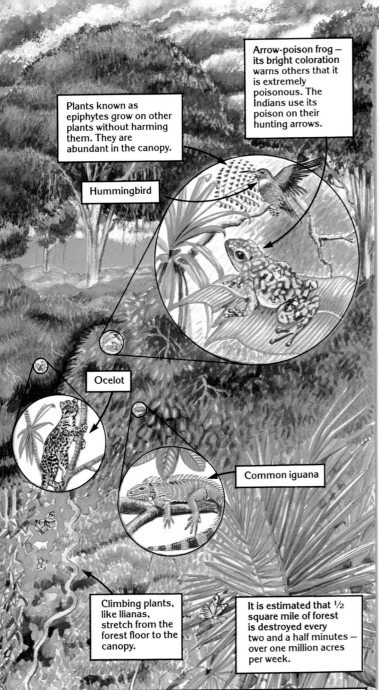

Plants known as epiphytes grow on other plants without harming them. They are abundant in the canopy.

Arrow-poison frog — its bright coloration warns others that it is extremely poisonous. The Indians use its poison on their hunting arrows.

Hummingbird

Ocelot

Common iguana

Climbing plants, like llianas, stretch from the forest floor to the canopy.

It is estimated that ½ square mile of forest is destroyed every two and a half minutes — over one million acres per week.

The forest floor is covered by several inches of fallen leaves. Here, organic matter is rapidly recycled by the decomposers, and minerals are transferred directly to shallow plant roots. This process is so efficient that the lower layer of soil has little mineral content and most of the forest's mineral wealth is stored in the vegetation.

When the forest is cleared and burned, the minerals stored in vegetation are turned to ashes. The root systems are destroyed, allowing rain to wash away the ashes and topsoil. The remaining soil soon becomes infertile, turning areas once rich in life into wasteland. It takes centuries for the forest to return, if ever.

People of the forest

The rainforest is home to many native peoples, who live in harmony with its environment. Their knowledge of the forest is very important to us, if we are to understand its workings and resources. But every day these people are being forced from their own lands with no regard to their wishes or basic human rights. Both they and their knowledge are being destroyed, along with the forests in which they live.

The importance of rainforests

Tropical rainforests play a vital role in regulating the world's climate, through their position in the oxygen, carbon and water cycles. They are the most important source of raw materials for new medicines and are a vital source of new foods (at least 1,650 rainforest plants could be used as vegetables).

We have hardly started to tap the rainforests' vast resources. However, this must be done in a sustainable way, that is, we must find a balance between making good use of the forest resources, like timber, rubber and nuts, and conserving the forests themselves.

Tapping rubber in the rain forest

Destruction of the rainforests

Almost 50% of the world's rainforests have already been destroyed, and the destruction continues. The underlying causes of this are the growing populations, poverty and unequal land distribution in countries with rainforests. This is made worse by the rich nations' demand for timber, and large, badly-planned aid programs. A long-term solution will only be found when these underlying causes are properly dealt with.

The result of forest clearance

Change in nature

Everything around us is constantly changing, from microscopic living cells to the landscapes in which we live. Some changes are rapid, others take millions of years. On these pages are examples of different sorts of change, both natural and man-made.

The changing landscape

For billions of years, great natural forces, like the earth's movement, volcanic activity, erosion and the rising and falling of oceans, have been reshaping the face of the earth and its environments. They are still doing so, but so slowly that it is hardly noticeable.

The features of Monument Valley (western USA) have been carved by erosion over millions of years.

More short-term changes in the natural world are known as **succession**. This is when a series of different plants and animals replace each other over a period of time until a **climax community** is formed. This is a community which will survive virtually unchanged if there are no disturbances in the climate, e.g. the tropical rainforests.

Succession resulting in a climax community.

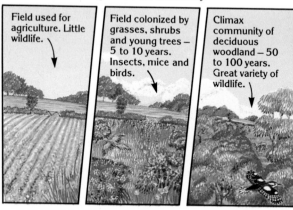

Field used for agriculture. Little wildlife.

Field colonized by grasses, shrubs and young trees – 5 to 10 years. Insects, mice and birds.

Climax community of deciduous woodland – 50 to 100 years. Great variety of wildlife.

The changes made by man to the earth's natural conditions can be seen all around us. In many places, farming, industry and urban developments have changed natural landscapes into man-made environments such as fields, towns and cities. Much of this has taken place over centuries, but increasing populations and industrialization in recent times have caused a dramatic increase in both the scale and intensity of these changes.

Changes in climate

The climate in different regions of the world changes throughout the year, according to the season. This is because the earth's axis is tilted while it travels around the sun. In tropical areas, with temperatures constant all year round, the amount of rainfall determines the season – dry or rainy. Further north and south, the climatic changes are much greater (especially in temperature), and there are four main seasons – winter, spring, summer and autumn.

The earth revolves around the sun at an angle, with its axis 23° off-center.

The angle of the sun's rays creates the difference in climate.

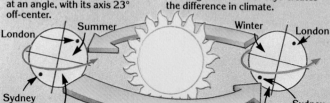

Summer in London will be winter in Sydney.

Photographing seasonal change

If you can get hold of a camera, try to take a series of photographs of the same natural scene over a period of time (perhaps the first day of each month for a year). The changes you will catch on film are fascinating. You could use them for a display, showing the variety of seasonal change.

The same scene in winter and summer

There are also more long-term climatic changes, which dramatically affect the earth's environment. Over the last 900,000 years there have been roughly ten major cold periods (ice-ages), with warmer weather between them. At present, it seems that we are in one of these warmer periods.

This graph shows the changes in global temperatures over a span of 900,000 years.

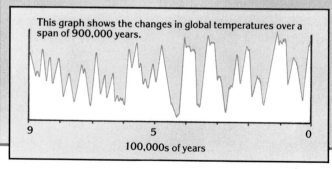

100,000s of years

Natural climatic changes take place gradually over thousands of years and so are no great threat to us at present. Of far greater importance is the danger that our large-scale industrial activity is changing the earth's climate. These changes will happen much more quickly and could well be much more dramatic. The greenhouse effect (see page 13), smoke and dust clouds blocking out sunlight, and the destruction of the ozone layer are all real threats.

Destruction of the ozone layer

High up in the atmosphere, a layer of ozone protects the earth from the sun's deadly ultra-violet rays, which cause skin cancer.

It seems that chemical compounds known as chlorofluorocarbons (CFCs), used in some aerosol cans and in making polystyrene and refrigerators, are gradually destroying this vital layer.

Some international action has already been taken to slow down the manufacture of CFCs, but many scientists want much more to be done.

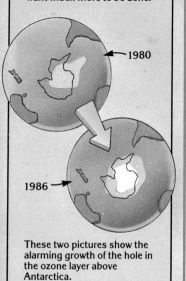

← 1980

1986 →

These two pictures show the alarming growth of the hole in the ozone layer above Antarctica.

Changes in living things

Everything in the living world is changing. Cells in all living things are constantly breaking down and being replaced by new ones. Individual plants and animals are produced, grow, reproduce and die – to be replaced by new generations. There are also great changes in life cycles and behaviour patterns whilst they live.

The seasonal differences in climates result in many changes in living things. Many animals adapt their life cycles to the changes in temperature and availability of food. Some **migrate** to other areas, often hundreds of miles away, where conditions are more suitable for feeding or breeding, or both.

The Arctic tern breeds in the summer on the shores of the Arctic ocean, then flies 12,500 miles to the Antarctic to feed during its summer.

It travels over 25,000 miles each year.

Many plants have adapted to seasonal changes by adjusting the times at which they produce flowers and seeds. Herbaceous perennials, for instance, die back at the end of each year, and leave just their underground stem and roots to survive the winter. Annuals survive the cold months as seeds. They flower and produce more seeds in the warmer months, dying off before winter.

Other animals, like snakes and hedgehogs, avoid the worst seasonal conditions by **hibernation**. They spend the winter months in a deep sleep, in which their body functions shut down to a minimum. Fat stored from summer feeding provides the little energy they need. **Aestivation** (or **estivation**) is like hibernation, except that it takes place where animals (like the African lungfish) need to survive very hot temperatures and drought conditions.

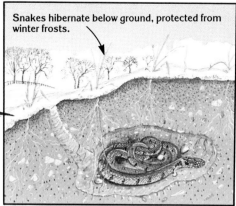

Snakes hibernate below ground, protected from winter frosts.

Daffodils are herbaceous perennials

Poppies are annuals

Watching butterfly metamorphosis

One of the most astonishing changes in the life cycles of living things is that from a caterpillar into a butterfly or moth, in a process called **metamorphosis**. To watch this, first build a container as shown in the diagram. Then find some caterpillars, placing them inside the box with a plentiful supply of the plant on which they are feeding (make sure this never runs out). At some point the caterpillars will transform themselves into pupae, from which the adult butterflies or moths will emerge. These should be let go as soon as possible.

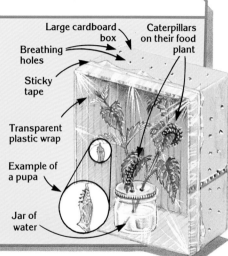

Large cardboard box

Caterpillars on their food plant

Breathing holes

Sticky tape

Transparent plastic wrap

Example of a pupa

Jar of water

Evolution

Living things have been changing and developing ever since life started around 3.5 billion years ago. This process of long-term change is known as evolution. By studying this and its link with changes in the environment, ecologists have learned a lot about the planet's workings. They have also seen how vital the links are between living things and their environment.

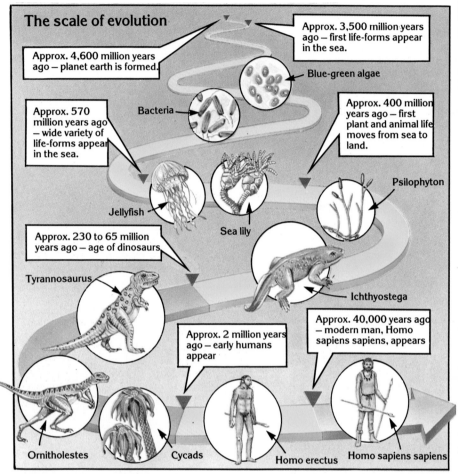

The scale of evolution

Approx. 3,500 million years ago – first life-forms appear in the sea.

Approx. 4,600 million years ago – planet earth is formed.

Blue-green algae

Bacteria

Approx. 570 million years ago – wide variety of life-forms appear in the sea.

Approx. 400 million years ago – first plant and animal life moves from sea to land.

Psilophyton

Jellyfish

Sea lily

Approx. 230 to 65 million years ago – age of dinosaurs.

Tyrannosaurus

Ichthyostega

Approx. 40,000 years ago – modern man, Homo sapiens sapiens, appears

Approx. 2 million years ago – early humans appear

Ornitholestes

Cycads

Homo erectus

Homo sapiens sapiens

The development of a human embryo in the mother's womb can be seen as evidence of the process of evolution. In the nine-month period of pregnancy, it undergoes a complicated process of development, starting off as a single cell and finally being born as a complex human.

These changes mirror those that took place over billions of years, in which life evolved from tiny, single-celled organisms into the complex structures of today. At one point, the human embryo even develops tiny gill slits, showing the connection to our distant relatives of the fish world.

The development of a human embryo

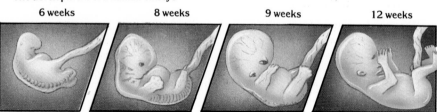

6 weeks 8 weeks 9 weeks 12 weeks

Fossils — a key to evolution

A fossil is the remains or the imprint of a plant or animal that has somehow been preserved in rock. Sometimes this happens when the shell or bone of an animal turns to mineral and thus its shape is preserved. Or the shape of the plant or animal is left imprinted in the rock, once its actual body has decayed away. The study of fossils, known as palaeontology, is one of the main ways we can find out about life in the distant past and how it has evolved.

Because they are found in specific layers of rock that can be aged, scientists can tell how old the fossils are.

By comparing fossils of different periods, we can see how life evolved.

Sometimes whole dinosaur skeletons are found fossilized.

Tools

Fossilized bones

A fossil hunter, or palaeontologist

Fossil hunting

Fossils are commonly found where sandstone, limestone or slate are exposed, though they are found elsewhere, too. All you need is a hammer and chisel and something to keep your samples in. Be observant when looking for fossils, as it is often very hard to spot the signs. Look for anything that seems out of place – different shapes, colors and types of rock. Use the hammer and chisel to break up lumps of rock to look inside. If you are successful, you could start your own fossil collection.

Here are some examples of what you may find:

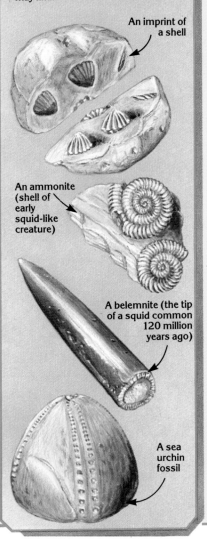

An imprint of a shell

An ammonite (shell of early squid-like creature)

A belemnite (the tip of a squid common 120 million years ago)

A sea urchin fossil

Darwinism

There are many different ideas about how the evolutionary process works. For the last 150 years, the theories of Charles Darwin have been accepted by most people as the best explanation. These depend on the idea of natural selection, or "survival of the fittest", to explain how living things have evolved into so many complex forms.

The natural selection theory states that the plants and animals that adapt best to their environment survive.

These then pass on their adaptations, which can include slight changes in physical structure, to the next generation.

In this way, living things can gradually change, or evolve, over long periods of time.

For example, smog in 19th century Britain made survival easier for dark colored peppered moths rather than silver ones, so more passed on their characteristics and their numbers increased.

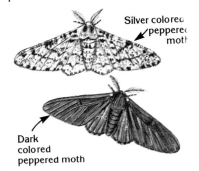

Silver colored peppered moth

Dark colored peppered moth

Beyond Darwinism

Some modern scientists think there are many things about evolution that Darwinism fails to explain adequately. They see natural selection as only one part of a much more complex process. Some think that evolution from simple cells into complex organisms shows that living things have an in-built tendency to organize their body structures and functions in ever more complicated ways. Whatever the truth, we are still a long way from fully understanding evolution.

The living planet

The earth itself has been changing over billions of years, too. In fact, life and the planet have constantly been evolving together, each affecting the other's development. For example, it was the early blue-green algae that, over millions of years, created the oxygen in the atmosphere, without which more complex life-forms would not have developed. Some scientists argue that the whole planet and its atmosphere works like a living organism. The idea of a "living" planet is known as the Gaia hypothesis, after the Greek Goddess of the Earth.

The planet earth seen from space – one vast living organism?

Man's responsibility

We now have the ability to create our own environments, and thus to control, to an extent, our future evolution. We also control the future of the earth and all that it supports. However, we are only just beginning to realize what a huge responsibility this is. There are many choices to be made and there is much to be done – some of our options are discussed in the following four pages.

People and planet

The human population is increasing at such a rate that both the environment and the balance of nature are threatened. This is one of the world's most urgent problems. But there are no simple answers, because it is the result of wide-ranging social, economic and political conditions which are all interconnected and which must be dealt with as a whole.

Population growth

It took thousands of years for the world's population to reach 1 billion*, sometime in the 1830s, but only another 100 years for the 2 billion mark to be reached in the 1930s. By 1975 the population had reached 4 billion and 12 years later it had grown by another billion, reaching 5 billion towards the end of 1987. It is thought that it will finally level out at about 10 billion towards the end of the next century.

This graph shows the growth, and predicted growth, of the world's population.

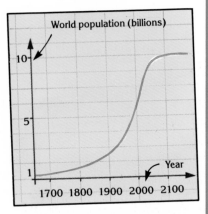

Most of this growth is taking place in the world's poorest countries, where the birth rate is greater than the death rate.

Population and resources

The earth has enough resources to support its population of 5 billion and more. But at present this is not happening. Millions of people in the poor world are living in hunger and poverty. The population problem is not so much "too many people" or "not enough land", as not managing to properly feed and support the growing populations.

Population problems do not necessarily come from a shortage of land:

Holland has a high population density but no problem, because it can afford to feed its population. India and Brazil have more land per person, but have a problem because they are poor.

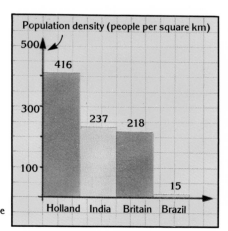

A major part of the problem is the unequal sharing of the earth's resources between the rich and poor nations, and between the rich and poor people within those nations. The average American born today, for example, will use 40 times as much of the earth's resources (e.g. food, fossil fuels, metals, etc.) as their equivalent in a poor African country. One cause of this is the unfair system of international trade, in which poor nations are forced to compete with each other to produce and export crops (like coffee) more and more cheaply, to the benefit of the rich nations.

The world is roughly divided into north and south in terms of wealth (annual income per person).

Rich world

Poor world

The great Indian leader, Mahatma Gandhi, once said: "The world contains enough for everyone's need, but not for everyone's greed."

Population and the environment

Many of the world's major ecological threats, like desertification (page 16) and rainforest destruction (page 27), are not necessarily caused by growing populations. The international economy, controlled by the wealthy nations, is also partly to blame. Many poor farmers are pushed off the best land, which is then used to grow export crops for the rich countries. They are forced to use poorer land or clear forest to produce the food they need to survive. To stop the environmental damage that this causes, there need to be changes in both national and international economic policies. The rich nations are the ones who can influence these policies, and so they control the future of the poor nations and their environments.

* These figures are based on the American billion, i.e. 1,000,000,000 (in other countries, e.g. Britain, one billion = 1,000,000,000,000).

Energy and the environment

Energy is vital for many of our basic needs, like cooking, heating and transport. Its production has a big influence on the environment we live in, so we must choose carefully the sources of energy that are to be used in the future. The choices that we make now will determine what the society and environment of tomorrow will be like.

Today's energy

The wealthy nations depend mainly on fossil fuels (coal, oil and gas) to provide their energy. They also produce some by nuclear power (using radioactive uranium) and some by hydro-electric power (using falling water). But the methods used are now seriously damaging the environment, e.g. the burning of fossil fuels causes acid rain and the greenhouse effect, and nuclear power produces long-term radioactive pollution and waste (and the danger of accidents).

In poorer countries the main source of domestic energy is wood (oil is used for industrial and transport purposes). This, too, has resulted in major environmental problems, with widespread deforestation (cutting down of trees) and soil erosion.

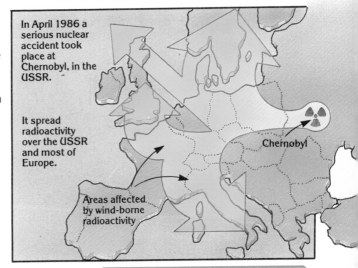

In April 1986 a serious nuclear accident took place at Chernobyl, in the USSR.

It spread radioactivity over the USSR and most of Europe.

Areas affected by wind-borne radioactivity

Chernobyl

Renewable energy

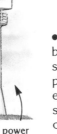

Safer and cleaner forms of energy production are now being introduced in many countries. These are known as renewable energy sources, as they will not run out, like fossil fuels eventually will. They are now being used successfully in different areas of the world and promise plenty of energy in the future, with far less risk to the environment. Below and to the right are some examples.

Wind power generator in Scotland.

● Solar power can be active (the use of solar panels to produce electricity) or passive (using more glass in buildings to trap the sun's heat) and has great potential, even in less sunny climates like those of northern Europe.

● Wind power is now being used for large-scale electricity production. It is especially useful for supplying remote communities and small-scale users.

● The use of specially planted, fast-growing plants and trees could supply local fuel needs.

● Burning industrial waste and urban refuse in smaller, more efficient combined heat and power (CHP) stations produces energy as well as solving the refuse problem.

Other sources include converting wave and tide energy into electricity, and the tapping of geothermal energy (the heat of the earth's core). There are some environmental problems with the use of some of these sources on a large scale, but these are minor when compared to the problems and limits of fossil fuels and the dangers of more nuclear accidents.

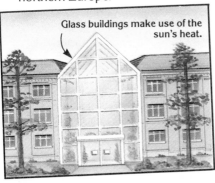

Glass buildings make use of the sun's heat.

Conserving energy

One way of lessening our use of fossil and nuclear fuels is to use energy more efficiently, so that less is actually needed. This can be done on a national scale – by saving energy used in industry and transport. But it can also be done at the level of the individual. Your actions, too, will make a difference. Here are some ideas:

Insulate your hot-water tank and pipes (as in the picture) – your water will heat up quicker and stay hot longer.

Don't waste electricity, e.g. turn off lights when not in use, have a shower or all-over wash instead of a bath (it uses less heated water).

Draftproof your doors and windows – this is simple to do and very effective.

Help your parents insulate the loft (if you have one) – this can save up to 20% of your energy bill.

The future

We are now finding ourselves faced with choices about the sort of environment that we want to live in. The main choice is whether to start working with nature, by understanding and working with its natural cycles, or to carry on working against it. The future of all the people in the world, and of the world itself, depends on the choices that we make today.

Solving the environmental crisis

Today, man's pressure on the natural world is causing a worldwide environmental crisis. Below are some of the main problems that we now face, along with some actions that we could take to improve the situation.

Soil erosion

Soil erosion occurs when the vital topsoil is removed in the wind and rain.

- reforestation (the planting of trees) – trees and hedgerows act as wind-breaks and their roots bind the soil.

- organic farming – organic matter retains water longer and binds the soil better, preventing it drying up and blowing away.

- smaller fields – the smaller the field, the more protected the soil will be.

Rainforest destruction

- reforms in land ownership in rainforest countries – to take the pressure off rainforest land.

- control of ranching and logging in rainforest areas, by lessening the rich world's demand for meat and tropical hardwoods.

- sustainable methods for using the forest's resources (methods that work with the natural cycles, and so can go on continuously), e.g. rubber-tapping.

Acid rain and other pollution

- pollution filters on power stations and motor vehicles.

- renewable energy sources.

- alternatives to artificial chemicals in farming.

- an end to pollution from industrial and nuclear sources.

Desertification

Desertification takes place when poor, arid land is over-used and turns to desert.

- less dependency on export crops in the poor world (these are grown on the best land, forcing poor people onto the more sparse land which soon turns to desert).

- appropriate irrigation techniques.

- more tree-planting schemes.

Destruction of habitats and wildlife

- more and larger wildlife parks in towns and countryside.

- stricter international controls and safeguards to protect natural habitats and prevent the killing and trading of wild animals.

Ozone depletion

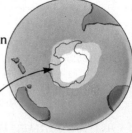

The protective ozone layer in the atmosphere is in danger of being destroyed.

- a complete ban on the production and use of chlorofluorocarbons (as soon as it is practically possible).

The greenhouse effect

- renewable energy sources.

- a halt to the destruction of the rainforest (these act as 'sinks', taking carbon dioxide from the air and using it up in photosynthesis).

- lower levels of energy use and wastage.

The wasting of our natural resources

- recycling of essential minerals.

- emphasis on building things to last and repairing them (rather than just throwing them away).

- better schemes to encourage us to change our wasteful lifestyles.

Practical action

All the suggested actions on the previous page must happen worldwide if they are to be successful. This demands much more international cooperation, especially between rich and poor nations. The trouble is that politicians tend to be more concerned with gaining support in their own countries in the short-term, than with the long-term future of the world and its people.

Many people believe that even all these actions will not be enough, and that we must all make very great changes in the way we live. They are working towards this in what is known as the green movement (see green politics, on page 45). This used to be called the ecology movement.

At the moment it is mainly charity organizations, like Oxfam, that are successfully helping the world's poor to help themselves.

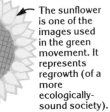

They give small-scale aid to communities, solving their problems without destroying local ways and traditions.

They use appropriate technology that the users can work and maintain, like this wind-powered pump in Africa.

The sunflower is one of the images used in the green movement. It represents regrowth (of a more ecologically-sound society).

The problems are worldwide, but we can all do something to help. Every small change you make to your life will mean that the overall situation improves. This book shows you some ways you can help – if you want to do more, contact the groups listed on pages 44-45.

Genetic engineering

One major problem that we are now facing is the control of genetic engineering. This is when scientists use living organisms (or parts of them) to change or create other life forms. They often experiment with genes, the parts of cells holding the genetic "code" that determines the characteristics of an organism.

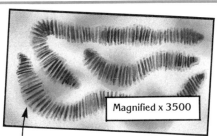

Magnified x 3500

By changing the information stored in the genes of an organism, scientists alter the characteristics of the new generation it produces.

Genetic experiments show how modern technology can be both a promise and a threat. For instance, some micro-organisms have been engineered to kill caterpillar pests, but some people feel that these organisms could seriously threaten the balance of nature. We need much stricter controls on such experiments than are now in use.

Antarctica – a test case

Antarctica is a continent almost untouched by the activities of man. However, many of the rich nations are now showing a keen interest in it, as it may hold huge reserves of oil and minerals. Other, poorer countries are also demanding a share. Environmental groups, like Greenpeace, believe it should be held in trust for the future as a world park. What happens to Antarctica is a test of our ability to cooperate now, in the interests of future generations.

Antarctica has a land surface greater than that of the USA and Mexico combined.

As a world park, Antarctica would be open to all for scientific research and protected from destruction.

Any oil pollution would seriously endanger the fragile ecosystem. The low temperature would drastically slow the breakdown of oil.

The holistic view

It is now very important that we learn to respect the natural world, not just because it supplies our basic needs (like food, water and air), but because it has a right to exist on its own merits. When we see that we are a part of this natural world, and not separate and above it, we begin to see the importance of protecting the great variety of living things it is made up of.

The holistic view looks at the natural world as an interconnected whole – the web of life – rather than a collection of many different parts. If we destroy separate strands of this web, we will end up destroying the web itself. If we do that, then we destroy ourselves.

Ecology projects

On the next few pages are some larger-scale projects that you could do, either alone or with friends, parents or teachers. They are all enjoyable and will help you learn more about ecology.

Building an ant observatory

For an introduction to keeping an ant colony, see page 20. Here you can find out how to make a formicarium, or observatory, to keep the ants in.

What you will need:

3 pieces of wood (15 in long, 2 in wide and over 1 in deep)

2 pieces of perspex or plastic (15 in by 17 in)

Some strong glue (for use on plastic and wood)

6 thin nails (2 in long) and a hammer

A piece of old stocking and a strong elastic band

Some garden soil, sand and leaf litter

A colony of ants

What to do

Take the 3 pieces of wood and, using the glue and nails, fasten them together in a U-shape as shown.

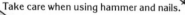
Take care when using hammer and nails.

Wait until the glue dries. Then take one piece of plastic and, putting glue around the outside of the wooden frame, stick the two together. Turn it round and do the same with the second piece of plastic on the other side.

Leave this to dry for a day or two. Now fill it with alternating layers of sand and soil (so the tunnels and chambers will show), topping it off with a thin layer of leaf litter.

Leave a 5 in gap at the top, to allow the ants some space. You could put in some twigs and leaves, too.

Collect the ants (try under large stones), using a soft brush and a jar – try to include the much larger queen ant. Empty them into their new home.

Give them some water (a moist lump of cotton), and some sugar, apple or other food-scraps. Secure the stocking or tea-towel around the top with the elastic band. Now watch the ants work.

Making a pond

One way to improve your environment and help local wildlife is to build a pond. To see what it might look like when completed, turn to page 5.

What you will need:

A spade

A very large sheet of plastic

Some large stones and some hay or straw

Old carpet or rags

Pond plants (grown in baskets) and pond weed

Plenty of water (rainwater is best)

A bucket of water, weeds and mud from another pond

Positioning

If you have a garden, putting in a pond will add interest. If you don't, you could try to find some land nearby, like school grounds or parkland, and get permission to build a pond there.

Keep the pond away from trees if you can, as falling leaves can be a big problem in autumn.

It is best to place the pond near some sort of cover, like a flower bed, hedge or rockery, as this will give frogs and toads some sort of protection.

Digging the pond

When making your own pond, you are free to design its shape.

Dig a hole at least 6 ft across and 1½ ft deep.

The sides should be gently sloping, with shelves at different levels.

Remove all the stones that stick out of the bottom and sides, and cover the bottom with old carpet or rags (this will stop anything puncturing the plastic).

Laying the plastic

Wash the plastic sheet thoroughly (to get rid of any chemicals still on it). Then lay it in the hole. Don't worry if it doesn't fit the contours exactly – the weight of the water will help.

Secure the sheet with large stones around the edge of the pond. You could use paving stones for this.

Place a 4 in layer of soil over the bottom of the pond (using some of the earth that you have just dug up). This will give plants a good base to grow from.

Filling the pond

Using a hosepipe or buckets, fill the pond with water. Don't fill it right up to the top – leave 2½ to 5 in – or else it will overflow when it rains.

Add your bucket of water, weed and mud from another pond. This will be full of animals, plants and seeds and will help life establish itself in your pond much more quickly.

Place your plants in the pond. These should be indigenous (plants that grow naturally in your local area). To make it easier to arrange them, you should keep them in their in baskets. Use small stones to attach pond weed to the bottom.

Let the mud and soil in the water settle.

Place some larger stones on the bottom for shelter, and also near the edges to help animals get in and out.

Add some hay or straw at the bottom to encourage scavengers and decomposers.

You could place a dead tree branch sticking out of the water, to give birds somewhere to perch.

Keeping the pond

If the pond gets too murky, put in plenty of pond-snails. These clean the water by feeding on the tiny algae that can make it dirty.

A few leaves blown into the pond will be beneficial. They will decompose on the bottom, releasing minerals. But try to keep the pond free of too many, especially in autumn, as they will cause problems.

Larger animals, like toads, frogs and newts, will find their own way to your pond after a while. Keep an eye out for them, but be patient.

Unless you want an ornamental fish pond, don't add fish to your pond (especially if it is quite small). They are greedy predators and will eat the smaller pond life.

You may need to top up the water level in dry periods, as some water will evaporate.

Ecology projects

Building a compost heap

If you have a garden and enjoy gardening, a compost heap is a useful addition. Most soils will benefit from added compost, as it returns vital minerals that are used up in plant growth, and it is more natural than adding chemicals.

What you will need:

Organic waste from the kitchen (tea leaves, potato peelings, left-over food, etc. – but not meat scraps)

Organic matter from the garden (like cut grass, leaves and weeds)

A nitrogen "activator" (speeds up decay), like manure

Some soil

Plenty of water

Some planks (of the same length) and 4 wooden posts

A hammer and nails

A piece of old carpet or plastic sheeting

What to do

The first thing to do is to box in the site:

Find a spot for the heap – about 1½ square yards in size.

Firmly plant four corner posts. Use planks for the walls. Include gaps for ventilation.

You could use bricks, too. Make sure that it's stable and has ventilation gaps.

The bottom layer should be twigs and sticks. Then add alternating layers of garden waste, kitchen waste, compost "activator" and soil. ▶

Keep the layers moist by adding water, and pack them down firmly.

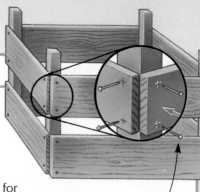

Take care when using a hammer and nails. Keep the nail straight and tap gently to begin with. Finish by hammering firmly.

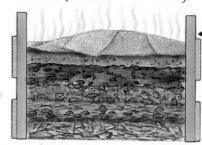

◀ When the heap is about 5 ft high, lay the old carpet or plastic sheeting over the top – this keeps in the heat.

Leave it for 5 to 6 months, keeping it damp throughout this time. You could start a second heap in the meantime.

Decomposers will break down the organic matter in the heap, creating a mineral-rich compost. This can then be added to your vegetable patch, flower bed or any other soil, and will help your plants to grow.

Sprouting beans and seeds to eat

Making bean and seed sprouts is easy, fun and supplies cheap and healthy food (they are a good source of vitamin C).

What you will need:

Some large plastic containers

Some beans or seeds from a shop, e.g. mung beans, cress, chickpeas or alfalfa seeds

Some pieces of muslin or old tea-towels

Some strong elastic bands

What to do

Clean out your plastic container – you could use a large yoghurt carton, or cut the top off a large plastic soft-drinks bottle and use the main body. Put in the beans or seeds, cover them in water and leave them to soak overnight.

Attach the muslin or tea-towel over the top with the elastic band and strain out the water. Leave the container and its contents in a warm, dark place overnight. The next day, take it out, wash the beans or seeds in water, drain them and put them back again. Do this each day and check their progress.

After 3 to 4 days, they should be ready to eat. Wash them and add them to a salad or use them as a sandwich filler – they are delicious and very nutritious.

Building a bird-table

Building a bird table and providing a regular supply of food will encourage birds to your garden, and help to keep them alive in the long winter months. For more information on feeding birds, see page 22.

What you will need:

A strong wooden post about 5 ft long.

A piece of wood 20 in square and 1 in thick

A hammer, nails and 4 strips of wood 18 in long

What to do

◄ One end of the post must be shaped to a point, to go into the ground more easily. Get an adult to help you do this, or buy one with a pointed end.

Carefully nail or tack the ► 4 strips of wood to the outside edge of the table-top, as shown here. These will stop the food from blowing away.

Remember: take care when using hammer and nails.

There should be small gaps at each corner to allow rainwater to drain.

◄ Nail the table-top to the top of the post (you could first drill small holes in the table-top for the nails, to prevent the wood splitting).

You could attach hooks from the sides to hang bags of nuts or other feeders.

Position the table where you can see it, but also where the birds can see cats when they approach.

◄ You could add a bird bath, too. Just fill an old baking tin or tray with a little water, and put it on the bird table. The birds will always enjoy a good bath.

One point to remember is that you should not really feed the birds in spring and summer, as there will be plenty of their natural food available. This is better for the young and growing birds than bread and kitchen scraps.

Birdwatching

Birdwatching is an interesting and enjoyable activity in both city and country, and can become a life-long passion. Try it and see.

What you will need:

A pair of binoculars are useful – of the many sizes, the 8 × 30 mm ones are light and powerful enough for most purposes.

A notebook, pen and colored pencils – for notes and drawings of what you see.

A small tape-recorder – for recording either bird song or a commentary of what you see.

A reference book to identify what you see.

Some helpful hints

The best time to see bird activity is just before dawn, though dusk is a good time, too. Midday is when there is least activity.

Birds are more active in the breeding season (spring and early summer) than in the nesting season (mid-summer onwards). Some are more active again in autumn as they prepare to migrate.

When stalking: keep quiet, move carefully and slowly, use cover and camouflage, and concentrate on the birds.

When observing: find some cover, get comfortable, keep still and quiet, and be patient.

Much of this advice is useful when watching other wildlife, too.

Ecology projects

Planting trees

On these pages you can learn how to choose, plant and maintain your own tree or trees. In doing so, you will improve the local environment and help wildlife by providing a vital habitat. Before you start, however, it is important you realize how much time and effort is involved. As well as the actual planting of the tree, there will also be several years of care before it can be left to itself.

What you will need:

A young tree (sapling) or trees

If you are growing trees from seed, you will also need: flower pots (or plastic containers with holes in the bottom), compost and a selection of tree seeds or seedlings.

A garden spade and fork

A strong wooden stake, about 5 ft long (only necessary if the sapling is over 3 ft high)

Wooden posts and protective wire fencing.

An adjustable rubber tie (from a gardening store)

Some mulch (wet straw, leaves, etc.) or peat

Planning your planting

To be successful, tree-planting must be carefully planned before anything is actually done. Several things need to be taken into account:

Where?

In your garden, your street, the school grounds, the local park or green, almost anywhere in fact. However, you will need permission from the relevant authority or landowner, unless it is your land. Make sure that nobody living nearby will object.

What sort of tree?

It is important to choose indigenous trees (those that are native to your area), as these will be better suited to the conditions and wildlife there. If you are planting near to buildings, roads or underground pipes, you should plant trees that don't grow too high. Their shorter roots are less likely to cause damage.

Will you need help?

Tree-planting is much easier if done by two or more people, though it can be done alone. If you are planting a lot of trees, or planting in public areas, it is best to get people from the local community involved. They can help by both planting the trees and looking after them afterwards. For advice, contact your local conservation group, council or gardening center.

Choosing your tree

The most satisfying way to raise saplings is to grow them from seed yourself, although this also takes the most time. Collect different types of freshly-fallen seeds in autumn and winter. Sow them in pots filled with moist compost, and wait for the spring. Some (like oak and beech) may germinate straight away, whilst others (like ash) won't germinate until a year later.

An acorn (seed) from an oak tree (native to Europe, Asia and North America) ▶

A beech nut and husk (native to Europe, though common in Asia and North America) ◀

A capsule (containing seeds) from a eucalyptus tree (native to Australia) ▶

The other option is to buy the young trees ready-grown from a local nursery or garden center. This can be quite expensive, though it will give more immediate results.

These are points to look for when choosing a sapling:

Well-balanced branches

Strong straight stem

Plentiful, undamaged roots (these should be kept damp)

The smaller the sapling, the easier it will be to transport and the quicker it will grow.

Take care when transporting. Trees can die of "shock".

How to plant your tree

When growing from seed, you should plant the young tree outside once it has reached 5-6 ins (see picture). It will need a lot of protection for quite some time, so should be planted in a sheltered, protected spot.

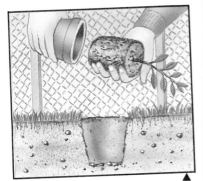

Dig a hole the size of your pot, loosening the soil at the bottom (to help drainage). Remove the sapling and compost from the pot, put it in the hole, and keep it well watered.

It might be necessary to protect it with a fence (as shown).

When planting a larger sapling, you will need to prepare the hole more thoroughly (see picture). Though if it is under 3 ft high, you won't need the supporting stake. ▶

Dig a hole the width of the roots and deep enough for the tree to sit in it up to its collar (where root and stem meet).

Break up the soil at the bottom of the hole with the fork.

Drive the stake (if needed) firmly into the ground, to about 15 in below the bottom of the hole.

Soak the roots well, ▶ and place the tree carefully in the hole. Shovel in some soil, shaking the sapling carefully to allow soil to get under and between the roots.

Firm gently with your foot. Add more soil and tread ▶ it down more heavily. Continue until the hole is filled and the soil is firmly trodden down.

The collar

Attach the tree to the stake with the rubber tie, and water the area well. Spread a layer of mulch or peat around the base of the tree (this prevents weeds from growing and also stops the soil drying up). ▼

If there is any danger of damage (e.g. mowing-machines or grazing animals), put up a fence around the tree.

Looking after your tree

For the first few years, the tree will need some care and attention.

If you are planting on public land, get the local community interested, as they could help in maintaining and protecting the trees.

Make sure the tree is watered, especially in dry periods.

Keep the ground at its base as free of plants and grass as you can (they compete for water and minerals), but avoid chemical weedkillers.

Adjust the rubber tie and repair the stake and fencing when necessary.

It is important to remember, when choosing, planting and maintaining trees, that they should be treated carefully. Trees are complex living organisms and are easily damaged and killed. If well planted and maintained, they will give people pleasure, as well as providing food and shelter for wildlife.

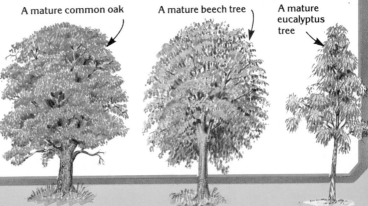

A mature common oak

A mature beech tree

A mature eucalyptus tree

Ecology projects

Making recycled paper

What you will need:

Old newspaper

Wire mesh (from a garden centre or hardware store)

Some absorbent cloths

2 buckets or bowls

Wooden spoon or liquidizer

Powder paint (to make colored paper)

Plastic bag

Weights, e.g. heavy books

What to do

Soak some old newspaper in a bucket overnight. The next day, drain off the extra water. Using the liquidizer (with permission if necessary) or your wooden spoon, mash up the paper and water into a pulp (and clean the liquidizer afterwards). Mix in the paint if you want colored paper.

Put the pulp into another bowl and add an equal volume of water. Mix these together. Slide the wire mesh into the mixture, lifting it out covered in pulp.

A windowsill salad garden

What you will need:

Plastic margarine tubs

Peat-based seed compost

Some seeds (e.g. radish, parsley, spring onion, mint, etc.)

What to do

Fill the tubs with compost to within ½ in of the rim, and firm this down. Plant the seeds under ½ in of compost and water them. Place them on a windowsill in the kitchen, and water them once or twice a week. Herbs like mint or parsley can be used to flavor cooking (cut off small pieces with scissors when needed), and the radishes or spring onions can be pulled up and used in salads. You could then start growing other herbs (like basil, sage and thyme) or perhaps lettuce or a miniature tomato plant.

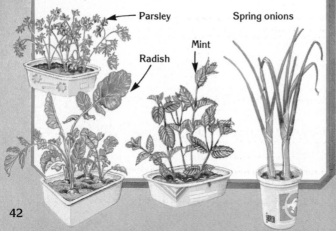

Parsley

Spring onions

Mint

Radish

Organizing your own group

If there is something you feel particularly strongly about (like cleaning up the litter in your area), you could try setting up a group to do something about it. The example here shows how you might create a pocket park on a piece of wasteland (see also page 25).

First, talk to your friends and see if they want to join in and help. Then try putting up notices or posters at school or in the library, telling people about what you want to do and how to contact you.

Prepare for your first meeting by noting down points for discussion, and ideas for action. It might be useful to invite an expert to give a talk or offer advice.

At the meeting, choose who is the chairperson (to make sure the meetings run smoothly), the secretary (to record decisions and inform members of future events) and the treasurer (to be in charge of money and accounts). You should also cover the first steps to take:

1 Find out who the land belongs to (ask your local authority), so you can get permission for your project.

2 Raise some money for things you may need to buy, e.g. seeds and shrubs. You could do odd jobs, or organize a raffle or sponsored walk.

3 Find out what help is available from the local authority or conservation group, and see what garden tools you can borrow.

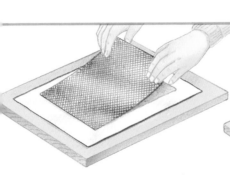

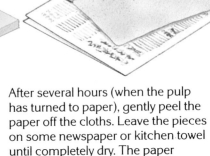

Lay a cloth on a clean, flat surface. Place the mesh (with the pulp side down) quickly and carefully onto the cloth. Press it down hard, then peel off, leaving the pulp on the cloth. Put another cloth on top and press down firmly.

Repeat these steps with your remaining pulp and cloths. When this is done, place the plastic bag on the top and weight the pile down.

After several hours (when the pulp has turned to paper), gently peel the paper off the cloths. Leave the pieces on some newspaper or kitchen towel until completely dry. The paper should now be ready for use.

Decide what each group member should do, and set a date for the next meeting.

Try to interest other people in what you are doing – get group members to write to the local papers, or put up notices or posters in libraries, schools and community or youth centers. Show how your work will improve the local environment and help its wildlife.

This is a poster about a canal clearing project. Try designing a poster about a pocket park.

You should have regular progress meetings until you are ready to start work on the site. Plan the layout, including perhaps a pond (see pages 36-37), some meadow (page 23) and plenty of trees (pages 40-41). Also, arrange to get rid of any large pieces of rubbish from the site (contact your local authority).

Working on your pocket park

1. Clear the ground of all rubbish, bricks and rubble.

2. If there is no topsoil, you can order it from a garden center. Mix it in with the soil already on the site.

3. After preparing the soil (digging it up, especially where it is compacted, and perhaps adding topsoil), plant plenty of seeds from different types of grass and wild flowers.

4. Make sure that you only use indigenous (native) plants, as these will support far more wildlife.

After everything is planted, you should keep working at the site – it will need to be maintained for quite some time (e.g. keeping it free of rubbish and protecting the young plants). All this hard work will certainly be worthwhile, once the park is set up.

If you want to get involved but don't fancy setting up your own group, you could join an environmental or conservation group. Many have their own local groups which organize activities, and they are always interested in new members (see addresses overleaf).

Going further

Below are some addresses of environmental, conservation and Third world development groups from around the world. Some are campaign groups (spreading information and influencing public, business and government actions), while others are involved in conservation work (like creating, maintaining and improving natural sites). Most have local groups which you can join.

Finding a local group

One way to find a local group is to check in your local telephone directory, under the heading "charities". Another method is to ask at your local library for information on local groups. But the best way to find out is to write to the organization's central office (some addresses are given below) and ask them whether there is an active group in your area.

International organizations

Friends of the Earth (FOE) – campaigns for protection of wildlife and habitats, and improvement of the environment at local, national and international levels. Youth section called Earth Action.

366 Smith Street, Collingwood VIC 3066, Australia

53 Queen Street, Room 16, Ottawa, ONT K1P 5CS, Canada

26-28 Underwood Street, London N1 7JQ, England

PO Box 39-065, Auckland West, New Zealand

530 7th Street SE, Washington DC 20003, USA

World-Wide Fund for Nature (WWF) (formerly World Wildlife Fund) – campaigns to protect wildlife and habitats throughout the world. Uses education to show the importance of the world's natural resources.

Level 17, St Martin's Tower, 31 Market Street, GPO Box 528, Sydney NSW 2001, Australia

35 Taraniki Street, PO Box 6237, Wellington, New Zealand

60 St Clair Avenue East, Suite 201, Toronto, ONT M4T 1N5, Canada

Panda House, Weyside Park, Godalming, Surrey GU7 1XR, England

1250 24th Street NW, Washington DC 20037, USA

Intermediate Technology – works on long-term development in poor countries, using technology appropriate to the needs of the rural poor. Aims to help people to become more self-reliant.

103-105 Southampton Row, London WC1B 4HH, England

777 United Nations Plaza, New York NY 10017, USA

Greenpeace – uses peaceful but direct action to defend the environment. Campaigns to: save the whales (see opposite), oppose nuclear power and weapons, stop acid rain and protect Antarctica.

134 Broadway, 4th Floor, Broadway, NSW 2007, Australia

Nagel House, 5th Floor, Courthouse Lane, Auckland, New Zealand

427 Bloor Street West, Toronto, ONT M5S 1X7, Canada

30-31 Islington Green, London N1 8XE, England

1611 Connecticut Avenue NW, Washington DC 20009, USA

Oxfam – involved in practical, long-term improvement of agriculture, health-care and social conditions in poor countries, as well as giving vital short-term emergency aid where and when it is needed most.

Community Aid Abroad, 156 George Street, Fitzroy, VIC 3065, Australia

251 Laurier Avenue West, Suite 301, Ottawa, ONT K1P 5J6, Canada

274 Banbury Road, Oxford OX2 7DZ, England

115 Broadway, Boston, MASS 02116, USA

Survival International – campaigns to protect surviving native peoples and the environments in which they live. Publicizes the risks to native peoples, and campaigns for their basic human rights around the world.

310 Edgware Road, London W2 1DY, England

2121 Decatur Place NW, Washington DC 20008, USA

National organizations

These organizations cover a variety of areas, including the environment, conservation and the Third World. Many will have local groups that you can join. If you are interested in further action, write to any of the addresses given here (including a stamp for return postage) and ask for information.

Australia

Australian Conservation Foundation, GPO Box 1875, Canberra, ACT 2601

Centre for Appropriate Technology, PO Box 795, Alice Springs, Northern Territory 5750

Rainforest Information Centre, PO Box 368, Lismore, NSW 2480

Total Environment Centre, 18 Argyle Street, Sydney, NSW 2000

The Wilderness Society, PO Box 188, Civic Square, Canberra, ACT 2608

New Zealand

Environmental Council, PO Box 10-382, Wellington

Nature Conservation Council, PO Box 12-200, Wellington

Royal Forest and Bird Protection Society, PO Box 631, Wellington

Tree Society, 41 Masterton Road, Rothesay Bay, Auckland 10

Canada

Canadian Nature Federation,
453 Sussex Drive, Ottawa, ONT K1N 6Z4

Ecology Action Centre,
1657 Barrington Street, Suite 520, Halifax,
Nova Scotia, B3J 2A1

Energy Probe / Probe International,
100 College Street, Toronto, ONT M5G IL5

Forests for Tomorrow,
355 Lesmill Road, Don Mills, ONT M3B 2W8

Sea Shepherd Conservation Society,
PO Box 48446, Vancouver BC V7X 1AZ

Society Promoting Environmental
Conservation,
2150 Maple Street, Vancouver BC V6J 3T3

Young Naturalist Foundation,
56 The Esplanade, Suite 306,
Toronto, ONT M5E 1A7

United Kingdom

British Trust for Conservation
Volunteers (BTCV),
36 St. Mary's Street, Wallingford,
Oxfordshire OX10 0EU

The Living Earth,
86 Colston Street,
Bristol BS1 5BB

Men of the Trees, Turns Hill Road,
Crawley Down, Crawley,
West Sussex RH10 4HL

The National Trust, PO Box 12,
Westbury, Wiltshire BA13 4NA

Royal Society for the Protection of
Birds (RSPB),
The Lodge, Sandy, Bedfordshire SG19 2DL

Scottish Conservation Projects,
70 Main Street, Doune, Perthshire FK16 6BW

WATCH, 22 The Green,
Nettleham, Lincoln LN2 2NR

United States

Defenders of Wildlife,
1244 19th Street NW,
Washington DC 20036

Food First,
1885 Mission Street,
San Francisco, CA 94103

National Audubon Society,
950 3rd Avenue,
New York NY 10022

Rainforest Action Network,
466 Green Street, Suite 300,
San Francisco CA 94133

Sierra Club,
330 Pennsylvania Avenue NW,
Washington DC 20005

The Wilderness Society,
1400 Eye Street NW,
Washington DC 20005

Greenpeace — saving the whales

One of the most famous campaigns by an environmental group was that of Greenpeace, when they attracted the attention of the world to the fate of whales in the 1970's. Some species, including the humpback, blue, fin and sperm whales, had been hunted to the edge of extinction, and whaling was still going on unchecked. Greenpeace activists confronted the whalers, preventing them from harpooning the whales. Their actions were captured on film, and shown to millions around the world on television news or in the papers.

The media coverage given to these actions resulted in growing public pressure to ban whaling. This, in turn, led to the 1982 decision of the International Whaling Commission (IWC) to ban commercial whaling for five years from 1985. However some countries have continued whaling since then, though on a smaller scale. Greenpeace are continuing their campaign against these whaling nations. They believe that after 50 million years of peaceful existence in the oceans, whales have earned the right to survive in peace.

By getting their inflatable craft between the whale and the harpoonist, the activists save the whale from a painful death.

Green politics

Many people believe that we must all make major changes in the way we live our lives if we are going to save the planet and ourselves from a harsh and difficult future. This view is put forward by "green" political parties all over the world, many of which are represented in their national parliaments. The West German green party (die Grünen), for example, increased their number of seats from 27 to 42 (out of 520) in the 1987 elections.

The green parties claim to offer an alternative to the usual political choices of the left, the centre or the right. They propose such things as a fairer sharing of the world's resources between rich and poor nations, and have far-sighted plans for the rebuilding of a new and better society. They believe that all governments should place people, the environment and the quality of life at the top of their list of priorities when making policy decisions.

Glossary

Acid rain. Rain and snow containing toxic chemicals which enter the atmosphere as industrial and vehicle pollution. It kills many living things, especially trees and freshwater plants and animals, and damages buildings and health.

Adaptation. The process by which living things adjust to their environment.

Aestivation (or **estivation**). A state in which body functions slow right down, to allow an animal to survive a period of intense heat or drought.

Appropriate technology. Tools, machinery and methods that are suitable for use and maintenance by the people that they aim to help (e.g. hand tools rather than tractors that need oil and spare parts).

Atmosphere. The mixture of gases which make up the air surrounding the earth.

Balance of nature. A state of equilibrium, or balance, between all things in nature (e.g. between living things and the environment).

Biome. One of the large **ecosystems** into which the earth's land surface can be divided. Each is the **climax community** of a region with a particular **climate**.

Biosphere. The global **ecosystem**, composed of the earth's surface, its waters, atmosphere and all the living things it supports.

Camouflage. The use of color or patterns by a plant or animal in order for it to merge into its surroundings.

Carnivore. An animal (or sometimes a plant) that feeds on animals.

Catalytic converter. A device fitted to motor vehicle exhaust pipes which extracts the harmful gases from the engine's exhaust.

CFCs (chlorofluorocarbons). Chlorine-based compounds, used mainly in aerosols, refrigerators and polystyrene, which are thought to be responsible for the slow destruction of the **ozone layer**.

Climate. Large-scale weather conditions (e.g. temperature, wind and humidity) that are characteristic of a certain region.

Climax community. A **community** that remains virtually unchanged, as long as there are no climatic or environmental changes.

Combined heat and power stations (CHPs). Smaller, more efficient power stations that are built in urban areas. They use heat produced by electricity generation to heat local houses, schools, etc.

Commensalism. A relationship between two animals of different **species** in which one lives off the food of another.

Community. The plants and animals within a certain **habitat**.

Conservation (of energy). Saving energy through increased efficiency and other methods, e.g. insulation (note this is different from conservation of energy in physics).

Conservation (of nature and wildlife). The protection and management of the natural world (animals, plants and **habitats**).

Consumer. An organism that feeds on other organisms.

Crop rotation. A farming method in which different crops are grown in one field each year over a four or five year cycle. This avoids the build-up of pests and the depletion of minerals in the soil.

Decomposer. An organism that lives by breaking down dead bodies, releasing the minerals they contain into the environment.

Deforestation. The cutting down of trees, mainly for fuel or timber, or to clear the land for farming or settlement.

Desertification. The process by which **marginal land** (traditionally used for grazing by poor peasant peoples) is transformed into useless desert by poor irrigation schemes, overgrazing and other over-intensive farming methods, or by a change in **climate**.

Development. The process of improving conditions in poorer nations through economic policies. Many people believe this only creates more problems, and want a return to traditional, community ways.

Dormant. Inactive (e.g. like a **hibernating** animal).

Ecological pyramids. Pyramid-shaped diagrams showing numbers, mass and levels of energy at different levels in a **food web**.

Ecology. The study of the interactions between living things, and between living things and their **environment**.

Ecosystem. A virtually self-contained system, consisting of a **community** of plants and animals in a given **habitat**, together with their non-living **environment**.

Energy. The basic requirement of all living things, giving them the ability to function. Originating as energy in sunlight and turned into chemical energy by plants through **photosynthesis**.

Environment. Everything, both living and non-living, that surrounds and affects an organism.

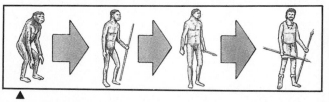

Evolution. The long-term process of change in organisms, often taking place over millions of years.

Export crops. Plants, like coffee, peanuts and cotton, that are grown mainly to be sold abroad. Poorer countries often depend on exporting these as their only source of income, to such an extent that not enough food is grown to feed local people.

Extinction. The dying out of a **species** of living thing, and hence its complete disappearance from the earth. Extinction is forever.

Food chain. A chain of organisms through which energy is passed, normally because they feed on each other.

Food web. A combination of **food chains** which connects all the living things within an **ecosystem**.

Gaia hypothesis. The idea that the earth is a "living planet", working as one vast organism.

Genes. The parts of cells in an organism that store information about its characteristics, ready to be passed on to the next generation.

Genetic engineering. Altering **genes** to create organisms that are useful to man. Can create dangerous new organisms.

Green movement. A loose grouping of many people with wide-ranging aims (peace, protecting the environment, etc), banded together to encourage social and political change in society.

Greenhouse effect. The build-up of gases in the atmosphere (mainly carbon dioxide, but also methane and others), trapping the sun's heat and thus affecting the **climate**.

Habitat. A specific area that is inhabited by plants and animals.

Herbivore. An animal that feeds on plants.

Hibernation. A state in which the functions of the body slow right down to allow an animal to survive periods of intense cold.

Holistic view. A view of the world as one vast inter-connected system, which cannot really be understood when studied as a mass of parts.

Indigenous. Belonging naturally to a particular area.

Intensive farming. Farming by methods that are unnatural, e.g. the use of artificial fertilizers, insecticides and other chemicals, and the growing of the same crop in the same field each year. These harm the soil (e.g by causing **soil erosion**), plants, **natural cycles** and possibly people.

Irrigation. The watering of land, mainly by using channels or ditches. Bad irrigation methods can make the land infertile, by bringing up too much salt to the topsoil (known as salinization).

Layering. The existence of different levels within a **habitat**, each with its own specific plant and animal life.

Marginal land. Land that is only just good enough for agriculture or grazing animals.

Mimicry. A form of **camouflage**, in which animals copy (mimic) the appearance or behavior of other animals or their surroundings.

Natural cycles. The processes by which the earth's elements are constantly recycled through living things and the **environment**.

Natural selection. An evolutionary process by which organisms that are most suitably adapted to their **environment** survive and prosper, while those that are not well adapted die out.

Niche. The position of an organism within its **ecosystem**, including its activities and relationships with other organisms.

Omnivore. An animal that feeds on both plants and animals.

Organic. Anything which is or was part of an organism (contains the element carbon).

Organic farming. The use of farming methods that work with nature's cycles, e.g. using **organic** waste from farm animals as fertilizer, natural pest and weed control and **crop rotation**.

Ozone layer. The upper layer of the earth's atmosphere, containing ozone gas which blocks out the sun's harmful ultra-violet rays.

Parasitism. The relationship between two organisms in which one feeds on another without giving anything in return.

Photosynthesis. The means by which plants use the sun's **energy** to build carbohydrates from water and carbon dioxide, releasing oxygen in the process (light energy is changed to chemical energy).

Pollution. The contamination of an area with unnatural substances or an excess of natural ones.

Pocket parks. Small areas of land in towns or cities that are kept in a natural state as miniature nature reserves.

Population. The number of organisms of one **species** in a certain area.

Predator. An animal that kills and feeds on another animal (**prey**)

Prey. An animal that is killed and eaten by another animal (**predator**).

Producers. All green plants, which make food from simple materials via **photosynthesis**. The basis of all **food chains**.

Radioactivity. Rays and particles coming from a decaying element of matter (large doses cause cancer and death).

Recycling. The re-use of materials, rather than wasting them.

Renewable energy. Energy from sources that are constant and natural, like the sun, wind and waves.

Resources. The available supplies of a material, e.g. a metal or food.

Soil erosion. The process by which vital topsoil is lost (mainly blown away by wind or washed away by rain), due to such things as **intensive farming, deforestation** and poor methods of **irrigation**.

Species. A set of organisms that can be grouped together for classification, due to their similarity or ability to inter-breed.

Succession. The series of progressive changes in an area, with one **community** replacing another, until a **climax community** is created.

Sustainable development. The use of methods of development that do not interfere with **natural cycles** or damage the ecological balance of an area (also sustainable forestry, farming, etc.).

Symbiosis. A relationship between two organisms of a different **species** in which both gain in some way.

Territory. An area occupied by one or more organisms and defended against other organisms (especially of the same **species**).

Third world. A term used to describe the poor nations of the world, which are mainly in South America, Africa south of the Sahara and south-east Asia.

Trophic levels. Different layers of a **food chain**, each containing organisms which get their food and **energy** from similar sources.

Index

Aborigines, 16
Acid rain, 15, 46
– solutions to, 34
Adaptation, 16-17, 46
– urban, 24
Aestivation (estivation), 29, 46
Antarctica, 35
Ants, 20
– ant observatory, 36
Appropriate technology, 35, 46
Arctic, 17

Balance in nature, 13, 46
Behavior
– social, 20
– colonial, 20
– territorial, 22
Biomes, 8, 46
Biotechnology, 35
Birds
– feeding, 22
– bird-table, 39
– watching, 39
Butterflies, rearing, 29

Cacti, 16
Camouflage, 17, 46
Canopy, 26
Carbohydrates, 7
Carbon cycle, 12
Carnivores, 9, 46
Catalytic converter, 15, 25, 46
Chemicals in farming, 15
Chlorofluorocarbons (CFCs), 29, 46
Climate, 6, 46
– changes in, 28-29
Climax communities, 28, 46
Colonies, 20
Combined heat and power
  stations (CHPs), 33, 46
Commensalism, 21, 46
Community, 5, 46
Compost heap, 14, 38
Coniferous forest, 8, 18-19
Conifers, identification, 19
Conservation (of energy), 33, 46
Conservation (of nature), 23, 46
Conservation groups, 44-45
Consumers, 7, 8-9, 46
Co-operation, 21
Crop rotation, 15, 46
Cycles, see Natural cycles

Darwin, Charles, 31
Deciduous forest, 8, 18-19
Decomposers, 8, 9, 46
Deforestation, 27, 33, 46
Desert, 2-3, 8, 16-17
– Australian, 16
– polar, 17
Desertification, 16, 46
– solutions to, 34
Dust-bowl, 7

Ecological pyramids, 9, 46
Ecosystem, 5, 8-9, 46
Endangered wildlife, 23, 34
Energy, 6, 7, 8, 9, 33, 46
Environment, 4, 6-7, 34-35, 46
Environmental groups, 44-45

Eskimoes, 17
Evolution, 30-31, 46
Export crops, 32, 46

Farming, 15
Fishing, 11
– whaling, 45
Food, 7, 8-9
Food chain, 8-9, 46
Food web, 8, 46
Forestry, 18
Fossil fuels, 13, 15, 33
Fossils, 30
– collecting, 31
Friends of the Earth, 44

Gaia hypothesis, 31, 46
Genetic engineering, 35, 47
Grassland, 8
Great Barrier Reef, 10
Green movement, 35, 45, 47
Greenhouse effect, 13, 29, 47
– solutions to, 34
Greenpeace, 35, 44, 45
Groups,
– organizing your own, 42-43
– environmental and conservation, 44-45

Habitats, 5, 47
– marine, 10
– destruction of, 23
– protecting the, 34
Herbivores, 9, 47
Hibernation, 29, 47
Holistic view, 35, 47
Humus, 6

Ice-ages, 28
Indians, South American, 27
Intensive farming, 15, 47
Intermediate Technology, 44

Layering, 26, 47
Lichens, 21, 25

Maquis, 8
Meadow reserve, creating a, 25
Metamorphosis, 29
Migration, 29
Mimicry, 17, 47
Minerals, 6, 7, 13

Natural cycles, 12-13, 47
– disturbance of, 14-15
Natural selection, 31, 47
Niche, 22, 47
Nitrogen cycle, 13
Nuclear energy, 33

Ocean, 10-11
Omnivores, 9, 47
Organic farming, 15, 47
Oxfam, 35, 44
Ozone layer, 47
– destruction of, 29
– protecting the, 34

Parasites, 21, 47
Photosynthesis, 7, 47
Plankton, 10
Plant galls, 21
Pocket parks, 47
– creating a, 25, 42-43
Pollution, 14-15, 47
– marine, 11
– urban, 25
– test of, 25
– solutions to, 34
Pond, 5
– building a, 36-37
Population, 47
– animal, 22
– human, 23, 32
Poverty, 32
Predators, 22, 47
Producers, 7, 8, 47

Radioactivity, 33, 47
Rainforest, 8, 26-27
– destruction of, 27
– saving the, 34
Recycling, 14, 47
– your own paper, 42-43
Relationships, 20-21
Renewable energy, 33, 47
Resources, 32, 47
– saving, 34

Savannah, 8, 22
Seasons, 28
Seeds, 7, 17
– sprouting, 38, 42
Social groups, 20
Soil, 6-7,
Soil erosion, 7, 47
– solutions to, 34
Solar power, 33
Succession, 24, 28, 47
Sun, 6, 7
Super-organisms, 20
Survival International, 44
Symbiosis, 21, 47

Territories, 22, 47
Traffic calming, 25
Transport, 25
Trees, 18-19
– for energy, 33
– planting, 40-41
Trophic levels, 9, 47
Tropical rainforest, see rainforest
Tundra, 8, 17

Urban areas, 24-25
Urban wildlife, 24

Waste,
– recycling, 14
– burning of, 33
– solutions to, 34
Water cycle, 11, 12
Weathering, 6
Whales, 11, 45
Wind power, 33
World Wide Fund for Nature, 23, 44